River
Rescue

River Rescue

~~~~~~~~~~

Second Edition

Les Bechdel
Slim Ray

APPALACHIAN MOUNTAIN CLUB BOOKS

BOSTON

Book design by Joyce Weston
Sketches by Jan AtLee and Mary Trafton
Photographs by Slim Ray, except where otherwise noted
Cover photograph by Wiley/Wales (Durango, CO)

Published by Appalachian Mountain Club Books, 5 Joy Street, Boston, MA
   02108
Distributed by The Globe Pequot Press, Old Saybrook, CT 06475

SECOND EDITION

Library of Congress Cataloging-in-Publication Data

Bechdel, Les.
     River rescue / Les Bechdel and Slim Ray; photographs by Slim Ray.
   — 2nd ed.
          p.   cm.
     Bibliography: p.
     Includes index.
     ISBN 0-910146-76-4
     1. White-water canoeing—Safety measures. 2. Rafting (Sports)—Safety
measures. 3. Rescue work. I. Ray, Slim. II. Title.
GV788.B43 1989
797.1'22'0289—dc19   88-28639

The paper used in this publication meets the minimum requirements of the
American National Standard for Information Sciences—Permanence of Paper
for Printed Library Materials, ANSI Z39.48-1984.∞

Printed on recycled paper. ♻
Printed in the United States of America.

10 9 8 7 6 5

5. **Boat-based Rescue   87**
    Rescuing Boaters   87
    Rescuing Swimmers   88
    Equipment Retrieval   94
    The Telfer Lower   98

6. **Entrapments and Extrications   108**
    Entrapments and Boat Pins   108
    Entrapment Rescues   111
    Entrapment Rescue Techniques   113
    Recovering Pinned Boats   118
    Rigging   118
    The Force of the Current   123
    Haul Systems   124

7. **Vertical Rescue   139**
    Safety Considerations   139
    Rappelling   140
    Bridge Lowers   141
    Tyroleans   145
    Helicopters   152
    Helicopter Evacuation   156

8. **Organization for Rescue   163**
    The Rescue Process   163
    Leadership   166
    Rescue Priorities   167
    System Selection   167
    Team Organization   168
    If the First Attempt Fails   170
    Liability   171
    The Media   171
    Thinking the Unthinkable—The Failed Rescue   172
    Reactions   174

9. **Patient Care and Evacuation Techniques   176**
    The Initial Contact   177
    Drowning   179
    Hypothermia   182
    Shoulder Dislocations   184
    Evacuation Techniques   185
    Moving the Litter   190

Contents

FOREWORD   xi

PROLOGUE: TWO RESCUES   xiii

INTRODUCTION   xvii

1. **River Sense   1**
   Characteristics of Whitewater Rivers   3
   Hazards   4
   Rating the Rapids   12
   Preparation   14
   Scouting   18
   Leadership   20
   Saying No   21
   The "What If" Factor   21

2. **Equipment   23**
   Personal Safety Equipment   24
   Clothing   35
   Ropes   38
   Boats and Rafts   41

3. **Self-Rescue   53**
   Strainers   60
   Entrapment   60
   Holes   61

4. **Rescue by Rope   65**
   The Throwing Rescue   65
   Throwing Techniques   70
   Multiple Swimmers   75
   Tag Line Rescues   76
   Strong-Swimmer Rescues   81

This book is dedicated
to the memory of Rick Bernard.

10. The Professionals   195
   The Rescue Professional   196
   Some Rescue Considerations for Professionals   199
   Professional Equipment   200
   The River Professional   204

AFTERWORD   210

APPENDICES   211
   A: International Scale of River Difficulty   211
   B: Universal River Signals   213
   C: The Force of Water   214
   D: Useful Knots   214
   E: Cold Water Survival Chart   218
   F: First Aid Kit   218
   G: Ground-to-Air Signals for Survivors   219
   H: Cardiopulmonary Resuscitation (CPR)   223
   I: Symptoms of Hypothermia   225
   J: Patient Assessment System (PAS)   226

OTHER SOURCES OF INFORMATION   228

INDEX   232

ABOUT THE AMC   238

Foreword

In the past twenty years whitewater sport has grown tremendously. With that growth has come a vast improvement in both equipment and skills. High-quality factory-made products have largely replaced the homemade gear with which many of us began. Well-organized clinics run by clubs and commercial outfitters have largely replaced the informal "school of hard broaches and long swims," with today's beginners learning more in a month than we did in a year. It is now possible for gutsy newcomers to attempt runs in their first year which frustrated top experts in the 1960s and 1970s. This has led to the opening up of new rivers of incredible difficulty and to the performance of wild "hot dog" maneuvers not even thought of as recently as ten years ago. The skill level of the average paddler today is higher than ever before in all areas but one: the ability to make effective rescues.

The reasons for this are simple. Before the 1970s, when fiberglass boats were not as prevalent as they later became, one's career in whitewater paddling used to begin with a long apprenticeship in open canoes. The rivers may have been easy by today's standards, but an aluminum canoe with no flotation or special outfitting teaches respect for the river very quickly. Minor mishaps were common: almost every trip included a pinning or two, and everybody got to lend a hand. Concepts like leadership and skills like rope handling were thus part of everyone's introduction to the sport, and when something serious happened everyone was fully trained and ready to respond. Contrast this to the experience of today's paddlers: thanks to their superior equipment and training, they may become involved with Class IV to V whitewater without ever having seen a serious pinning. Problems in such rivers are often severe, but if paddlers have only a limited background to draw on, their response may not be equal to the challenge . . . unless the group has made an effort to acquire the needed skills elsewhere and in advance.

While the paddling public has become less involved with rescues, professional outfitters have refined their safety-and-rescue skills to a high level. Their intensive training, combined with the sheer number of inexperienced people they encounter, makes them the people to consult on the subject. The authors of this book, Les Bechdel and Slim Ray, have been leaders in this area for some time. Bechdel, a former national kayak champion and vice president of the Nantahala Outdoor Center who is now president of

Canyons Incorporated, won the Red Cross Certificate of Merit for his actions in one of the rescues described in this book's early chapters. Slim Ray, a talented author and photographer also associated with the Nantahala Outdoor Center, blends Bechdel's hard-earned wisdom with his own experience to produce a superior text. As a result, this book will be of great value to the advanced paddler concerned with developing rescue skills.

But remember: reading this book is not enough! If you wait until trouble strikes before you practice, as we did in the old days, you may find yourself with more than you can handle. Take time to develop these skills, either through informal training sessions or through clinics offered by established canoe clubs and professional outfitters. Doing so will increase your appreciation of the river and give you the confidence you need to tackle difficult rapids. And the added margin of safety will make your sport more enjoyable.

Charlie Walbridge
American Canoe Association safety chairman

Prologue: Two Rescues

A Drowning on the Chattooga

It was a trip like any other. After a high-water year the Chattooga had finally settled down to a medium level (about 1.8 feet), and we had started to relax a little. There were six rafts and a safety kayak on the trip. Rick Bernard, an expert paddler, had traded a raft-guide slot on another trip to be safety boater. It was a fine November day and we did not expect trouble. There were no problems moving through the Five Falls area, and when we reached Jawbone, the next-to-last rapid of the series, we waited for Rick to run through first. He decided to catch the eddy above Decapitation Rock, a huge undercut boulder about halfway through the rapid. This was common practice for safety boats, and Rick had done it before. The danger of the move is that this steep, small eddy flows out directly into the undercut end of the rock.

Rick caught the other eddies in the rapid nicely but hit the eddy above "Decap" low and began to slip back. We had seen this too; the boater must flip here deliberately to avoid hitting the rock with his head. As Rick slid under the rock, we watched the downstream side to see him roll. Nothing happened.

The next thing we saw was his hand reaching up from beneath the rock to try to find a hold. An alert guide threw a rope, but Rick was unable to hang on to it. After a few more seconds the hand disappeared. Shortly after that his life jacket washed out.

Rick's boat was pinned about a foot from the stern and folded underneath the rock. It was made mostly of nylon and other synthetic fibers that would not tear (a breakaway cockpit would have been of no use in this situation anyway), and the problem was compounded by the lack of footbraces. Since the boat was now facing downstream, the force of the current was pushing Rick against the front of the cockpit rim.

There were people on the other side of the river, including one of our rafts, but communication was difficult because of the noise of the water. It took several long minutes for them to understand exactly what the situation was. Even then, the rescue attempt was hampered by inadequate equipment. Rick's boat was barely visible from the top of the rock, and the whole force of the current slammed into the upstream side of the rock. We had ropes but nothing else, not even a carabiner, to hook onto the boat. The boat's grab loops were out of reach, and although I was able to reach and release his sprayskirt in the hope that the boat would fill up and wash off, I couldn't get a rope around the boat. We tried every method we could think of for over an hour, as hope for Rick's life faded.

Dave Perrin, the trip leader, had to think about the rest of the people on the trip. It was getting late and we were overdue. The guides ran the rafts through Jawbone and met the customers below. Dave appointed a substitute leader, and the trip set off for the takeout. At the same time he sent a runner out to notify our company of the situation. Since we expected help. Dave and I stayed there.

Just before dark Payson Kennedy (director of the Nantahala Outdoor Center), Andrew Stultz, Bruce Hare, and a member of the local search-and-rescue outfit showed up. With fresh people and ideas we renewed our efforts. We didn't want to leave our friend under that rock! Finally Andrew formed a coil of rope and dropped it in above the rock right where Rick's boat had gone in. The water sucked the rope in just as it had the boat, and the rope looped around the folded part of the boat. In the gathering darkness we secured the rope to the boat and passed it over to the other shore. Pulling directly against the current, it was all six of us could do to pull it out. It has taken us five hours to find the right combination for the recovery.

Slim Ray

Rescue on the Bío-Bío

In January 1981 three commercial rafting outfitters were making their way through the infamous Nirreco Canyon of the Bío-Bío River in Chile. Our group was scouting a quarter-mile-long Class V rapid called Lava South and had pretty much concluded it was too big for our paddle rafts. After constant rain the river was running more than 20,000 muddy cubic feet per second, and things looked ominous.

With another outfitter, who was camped below the rapids, we watched the third outfitter's rafts crash their way through Lava South. The size of the rapid made control marginal, and the rafts were barely making it into the eddy above the next rapid, Cyclops (another Class V).

As we watched I saw an emergency signal from one of our guides at the top of the rapid. A raft was coming through upside down and one of the passengers was backstroking weakly for the left shore. We lost sight of him for what seemed an eternity in the big waves. When he flushed out in the tail waves, he was floating face down.

Three of us—all employees of the Nantahala Outdoor Center: Dick Eustis, Drew Hammond, and I—were on a 15-foot cliff overlooking the fast current that led into Cyclops Rapid. We all saw what had happened, and each of us reacted differently: Dick dove into the water immediately. I followed, and Drew, who was farther downstream, began getting a throw rope ready. A boatman from the other company was already on his way to his oar rig to back up the rescue. Each of us acted on instinct, based on his position relative to the victim. There was no time for discussion, only action.

Dick swam to the victim and tried to give mouth-to-mouth resuscitation while they were both still in the water, but he wasn't successful in the big waves. I reached the victim, and we started swimming him in, using a sidestroke, with each of us holding a lapel of his life jacket to keep him on his back.

Drew made a remarkable rope throw, but it was a long one, and only Dick was able to grab the end. The force of the current on the three of us was too strong, so I let go and swam for it. Drew did a dynamic pendulum belay, running downstream as Dick and the victim swung across the eddy line.

John, a boatman from another company, was there in his oar rig, and he pulled the victim out of the water onto a large dry box. A quick check confirmed that the victim was not breathing. Dick started mouth-to-mouth resuscitation, and Drew began the chest compressions. In their haste they were initially out of sync, but John started counting and got things together for effective resuscitation.

His friends across the river couldn't help us but shouted that his name was Billy. Within a few minutes Billy started to vomit, and we had to roll him on his side. I checked his pulse at the carotid artery on his neck to measure the effectiveness of the compressions and then arranged for a backup CPR team.

After a few minutes of this Billy blinked his eyes and moved. We stopped CPR, he moaned, and by God he was breathing on his own! He started shivering violently but was still unconscious. We cautioned each other that we might have to restart CPR. We moved him from the raft to a tent with a caterpillar pass and began warming him under sleeping bags with our bodies. He regained consciousness that night and was able to walk the next morning.

In retrospect, it was fortunate that we were in the right place at the right time. But without the preparation, skill, and organization, that luck wouldn't have mattered.

Les Bechdel

Two stories. A drowning in one and a successful rescue in another. How and why did these events happen? These narratives give a firsthand account of what happens in a whitewater emergency. You may not understand now exactly what went on or why, but the purpose of the rest of the book is to answer those questions.

Whitewater is a challenging sport and the rewards are great, but the inherent risk of injury or death must be recognized. Too much that has been written about whitewater either ignores this danger entirely or overdramatizes it to impress the reader. We've tried not to do either. The safety of any adventure sport is directly related to the knowledge of and preparation for its hazards. You will better enjoy your sport if you are better prepared to deal with its dangers.

Introduction

Compared with other adventure sports, like skiing and mountaineering, white-water river sports are relatively new. Their history in the United States really begins just after World War II, when a small group of enterprising entrepreneurs began taking people down the Colorado River in rafts made from war surplus bridge pontoons. The real boom began in the 1960s when new designs, technology, and materials made possible the boats and inflatable rafts that we know today and opened up new rivers for exploration and recreation.

As with any new adventure sport, there were accidents and fatalities. River runners in general, and kayakers in particular, soon earned a reputation as daredevils, a reputation many of them were slow to reject. And in fact there was a great deal of danger on those early trips. Old-time rafters and boaters delight in telling stories of how things were in the old days and of the near misses. Some of the danger was caused by the primitive equipment of the time, but more of it resulted from people's ignorance of the dangers of the river and of the potential of rescue techniques.

As the sport's popularity increased in the 1970s many articles and books appeared, but they concerned themselves mainly with paddling technique and trip reports. In spite of a growing number of accidents, the literature of safety and rescue remained meager. It is to fill this need that *River Rescue* was written.

Some of the techniques mentioned in this book are simply the application of common sense. Others come from experience, both useful and bitter, and some are adaptations of proven mountaineering techniques.

We want to emphasize two things: first, that these techniques are still evolving and will continue to change and develop; and second, that it is important to share experiences and techniques with others. A problem today with discussing whitewater rescue is the lack of a central clearinghouse for collecting statistics, accounts of drownings and near misses, and descriptions of new safety and rescue techniques. All readers are encouraged to send accident reports, photos, or clippings of rescue- and safety-related material to the Safety Committee of the American Canoe Association (Box 248, Lorton, VA 22079). This information is assimilated into an annual report that is made available to paddlers nationwide.

Realizing that rescue systems and concepts of safety differ from one area of the country to another, we've tried to incorporate the systems and techniques that we have used and found to be effective. This doesn't mean that if a technique isn't in this book it doesn't work or shouldn't be used, just that we've used the ones we've described and know that they do work.

This book is not a "how-to-paddle" or a first aid book. We assume that the reader has a basic knowledge of whitewater paddling and knows some rudiments of first aid. We strongly recommend that all paddlers take a first aid course; it is essential for anyone who works or plays on a river.

Many things have changed on the river since we completed the first edition of *River Rescue* in 1984. One of the most disturbing trends is the recent increase in accidents and drownings among expert paddlers. On the bright side, however, safety awareness is higher than ever, especially among recreational paddlers, and things like carabiners, knives, and prusik loops are now commonplace.

Another positive trend is the sharing of knowledge among different areas of the country and the world, especially Europe. The international conferences on safety and rescue have allowed us all to benefit from each other's knowledge and experiences. There is still a lot of insularity and provincialism in the paddling world (usually expressed as "my way is the only safe way"), and we hope that the next few years will see a greater understanding of other paddling area and an appreciation of the different situations and problems in each.

This change has also been reflected in our personal lives. In the first edition we wrote that there was "no denying a certain Southeastern bias in this book." This has changed. Les now runs his own company, Canyons Incorporated, on the Salmon River in Idaho, and Slim was, among other things, the U.S. representative to the International Canoesport Safety Symposium in Mayerhofen, Austria, in 1986. Both of us have taught many rescue courses both nationally and internationally, which, we believe, has given us a unique perspective on the international rescue scene. Consequently, there have been some fairly major changes in certain sections of the second edition. We wish to thank all those who took the time to write with comments and suggestions (and encourage all to continue) and those we neglected to thank in the first edition, specifically Eric Nies, Susan Bechdel, Ciro Pena, Cindy Hilmoe, Dennis Kerrigan, Jeff Ward, Dick Eustis, Warren Berg, Jim Seggerstrom and Rescue 3, Whetstone Photography, Charlie Walbridge, Fran Manti, John Barbour, Kent Ford, John Dolbeare, Jan Letendre, Terry Hill, and all the good folks at the Nantahala Outdoor Center.

The face of the river, in time, became a wonderful book . . . which told its mind to me without reserve, delivering its most cherished secrets as clearly as if it had uttered them with a voice. And it was not a book to be read once and thrown aside, for it had a new story to tell every day.

MARK TWAIN, LIFE ON THE MISSISSIPPI

· 1 ·

River Sense

When something goes wrong on the river there seem to be two types of people: those who have foreseen the trouble and are already taking corrective steps—and the rest of us, who are standing there with mouths agape trying to figure out what's going on. The first type of person always seems to be just where he's needed at the critical time. Such people have "river sense."

People are not born with river sense; it's something they develop over time. It involves perfecting skills, understanding equipment, and appreciating the forces and hazards of whitewater. It involves an ability to evaluate other people's paddling skill, a sense of group dynamics, and effective communication with other people. It involves simply being alert at all times on the river.

River sense means accident prevention. Most river accidents and drownings are a result of a combination of poor planning, improper equipment, and plain ignorance. In the spring of 1984, for example, five rafters drowned after attempting to run a low-head dam on the Potomac River. Evidently they had no idea of the power of the deadly hydraulic at the base of the dam. Accidents of this nature can be prevented, and they are doubly tragic because they lead to unnecessary regulation by well-meaning public officials who often don't understand that there are better, less restrictive ways to save lives.

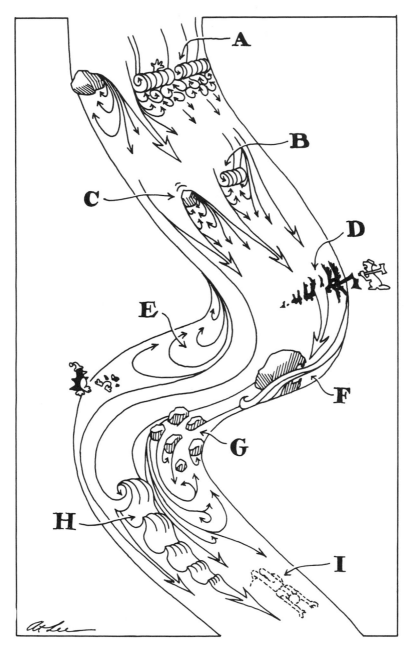

Fig. 1.1. River features and hazards: (A) ledge hydraulic, (B) hole, (C) rock with eddy below and pillow upstream, (D) strainer, (E) bank or shore eddy, (F) undercut rock, (G) boulder sieve, (H) standing waves, (I) submerged undercut rocks.

Characteristics of Whitewater Rivers

Four factors should be considered in assessing the difficulty of a whitewater river: elevation loss, volume of flow, geomorphic makeup of the riverbed, and hazards. Other factors, like weather and accessibility, must also be considered, but they do not, strictly speaking, define the difficulty of the river.

Elevation loss in the United States is normally expressed in vertical feet per mile, usually as an average figure over the section normally run: the net vertical drop between two points 1 mile apart. Averages can be deceptive, however, since some rivers concentrate their elevation loss in one steep section, thus hiding a difficult section with easy water before and after. For example, Section IV of the Chattooga has an average drop of about 50 feet per mile, but in the quarter mile of the Five Falls it averages well over 200 feet per mile. Rivers like this are called pool-and-drop rivers. Other rivers, like the Arkansas River in Colorado, have a steadier elevation loss. These rivers are often more dangerous, since they may have no calm pools in which to recover after a difficult section. Furthermore, there may be the risk of a long swim in cold water if things go wrong. Continuous Class III water may thus be more dangerous then pool-and-drop Class IV.

Volume of flow must be considered along with elevation loss in determining the difficulty of a river. Flow is measured in cubic feet per second (cfs): it is the volume of water that passes a given point on the riverbank in one second. Elevation loss and volume of flow are often inversely proportional: a big river like the Colorado will carry more than 20,000 cfs (it ran over 100,000 in the spring of 1983) through the Grand Canyon, yet the average drop is just over 8 feet per mile. Some of the scarier creek runs in the East drop almost 300 feet per mile but typically carry a scant 200–300 cfs. In general, the higher the numbers, the hairier the paddling. Right now the outer limits of navigability are represented by rivers that combine big continuous water with lots of elevation loss.

The riverbed itself partly determines the difficulty of the run. Narrow riverbeds may have tight turns and constrictions, and are more likely to be blocked by fallen trees, rock slides, or an intrusion of boulders from a side canyon. The geomorphic makeup of the riverbed will largely determine the presence or absence of undercut rocks, boulder sieves, potholes, and ledges. All create unseen hazards. Two examples of rivers with extreme geomorphic hazards are the Chattooga in South Carolina/Georgia and the Gauley in West Virginia (see figures 1.3 and 1.8).

The nature of the gorge through which the river flows also dictates the commitment a paddler must make. Paddling a river in a steep-walled canyon is a much more serious undertaking than paddling one that has a road alongside.

Fig. 1.2. A rescue at Bull Sluice. The rope thrower has thrown half the rope to the rafters and the other to a swimmer farther down.

Hazards

A whitewater hazard is any obstacle or condition that is capable of harming a boater. It may be a hard object like an undercut rock or a fluid one like a hydraulic. Most whitewater paddling can be looked at as the avoidance of hazards. To avoid them you should understand what they are and how they work.

Holes. The novice is often surprised to learn that not all surface water in a river flows downstream. Powerful upstream currents and waves in the form of eddies, hydraulics, and "holes" can be serious hazards under certain conditions (see figure 1.4).

An eddy is an upstream current that forms behind a surface object in the river or behind a riverbank. As the water flows around the object it piles up on the upstream side and then flows in behind the object, creating a reverse current. The line between the upstream and downstream currents is the eddy line. Larger and faster flows produce a marked difference in height between the upstream and downstream currents. Eddy lines in large, swift, rivers can themselves be a hazard as serious as any you may find on the river: they may be several feet wide and studded with crosscurrents and whirlpools.

Fig. 1.3. A geomorphic hazard: the Chattooga's infamous Bull Sluice pothole at very low water. Hazards like this are hard to see at higher water. A paddler drowned here in 1982.

ANY FLOATING OBJECT MAY
BE HELD BY BACKWASH

Fig. 1.4. A typical hole caused by water flowing over a rock.

Water also forms a reverse current when it flows over a submerged object such as a ledge or boulder, creating one of the most enjoyable but dangerous features of the river, the hole. There are many words for it (*pourover, hydraulic, stopper, reversal, sousehole*), but in this book we'll use *hole* to mean the general phenomenon of a reverse current that tends to trap and hold a buoyant object.

Small holes are great fun to play in with a decked boat. Boaters love to see who can go in the biggest one, stay the longest, and do the most stunts. But there are a few things to remember: don't stay in until you're exhausted, because getting out is harder than getting in. And look downstream before you go in: what's down there if you have to come out of your boat?

Large holes can be deadly and are capable of holding boats and boaters for extended periods of time. Smooth ledges with no breaks in them and low-head dams form the worst holes (see figure 1.7). This type of hole is often called a hydraulic. A hydraulic is frequently hard to see from upstream, and the regular nature of the backwash makes it nearly impossible to get out of without help.

Fig. 1.5. Some holes are great fun to play in, like this one on Section III of the Chattooga . . .

Fig. 1.6. . . . and some aren't, like this one at Sock-em-Dog Rapid in the Chattooga's Five Falls. Note the helmet of the boater swimming out just downstream of the boat.

BOIL LINE

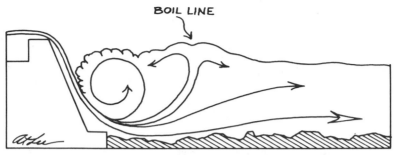

Fig. 1.7. A hydraulic caused by a low-head dam.

On bigger rivers, breaking waves can also form holes as the tops of the waves fall back upstream. Large ones are quite capable of flipping rafts and giving boats a thrashing, but they are generally less dangerous than hydraulics, since an upside-down raft, a swamped boat, or a person will usually flush through. However, mishaps like this often set the stage for worse things on a large, cold, continuous river.

Undercuts and Potholes. It's sometimes sobering to see a river at low water and realize what you have been paddling over when the water was high. The geological reasons for undercuts (large rocks that are narrower at the bottom than at the top) and potholes (smooth, eroded depressions in rocks; sometimes the rock will be worn right through to form a tunnel) are not important to the paddler, but their existence and location are (see figure 1.8). At higher water undercuts can often be recognized by the absence of an upstream pillow of water, and frequently they will have water boiling up behind them. The danger of an undercut is that a boat or a person can be pushed under it and trapped by the force of the water, pinning the boat or entraping an extremity. Undercuts also collect logs and other river debris, which form strainers and increase the risk of entrapment. The most dangerous undercuts are the ones on or near your line through a rapid, the ones the current pushes you directly into.

Entrapment. One of the biggest dangers of an unplanned swim in a shallow, rocky river is entrapment, a general term for getting any body extremity, usually a foot, or a leg, caught against the river bottom by the force of the current (see figure 1.9). Often a person unfamiliar with whitewater will attempt to stand on the river bottom and walk to shore. This is an invitation to get a foot caught in a tapered crack between two rocks or in an undercut ledge. Once the limb is caught, it is held there by the force of the current. Escape is difficult, and it is likely that the person will drown. If the river is fairly deep (more than about 4 feet) the chance of foot entrapment is smaller, unless the drops are very steep—in vertical or near vertical drops the swimmer is forced from a horizontal position to a more or less vertical one, which increases the risk of entrapment in a boulder sieve or rock crevice at the bottom of the drop.

Fig. 1.8. Another common hazard on some rivers is the undercut rock. An undercut is a likely pinning sport and should be avoided. (Photo by Robert Harrison/Whetstone Photography)

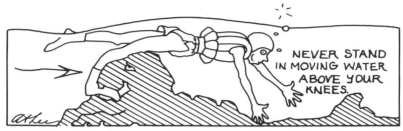

Fig. 1.9. Entrapment.

Left Crack of Crack-in-the-Rock Rapid on the Chattooga is a good example of a place where entrapment is a danger (see figure 1.10). The opening is very narrow and tapers down to less than the width of a person's body at the bottom. At higher water the crack fills in and the water will carry a swimmer over the deadly tapered section; at very low levels there is not enough water to carry a swimmer into it. At medium levels, however, it is a killer: the water carries the victim directly into the taper and wedges him there with the full force of the current.

Fig. 1.10. Left Crack of Crack-in-the-Rock Rapid is just wide enough to wedge a paddler's body in and hold it with the force of the water. The danger level is somewhat higher than the level in this photo.

Strainers. Fallen trees and accumulations of debris can form strainers: water flows through, but a solid object like a boat or a person won't. A strainer can completely block a narrow river. Strainers are particularly dangerous because they look so innocent. Frequently they are also hard to see, especially when a fallen tree trunk is stripped of branches and partly submerged. Not only trees are dangerous, though: smooth, water-worn boulders pushed down from a side creek can form boulder sieves at low water and trap boats and people or, at high water, form a series of hydraulics.

Fig. 1.11. Kayakers crossing a half-submerged log on Colorado's Piedra River. Unlike fixed hazards, such as low-head dams and undercuts, strainers can be a surprise, since they can be created or can move overnight.

In the summer of 1987 five people drowned when their raft struck a massive strainer on Canada's Ellaho River.

Debris. In addition to all the hazards nature has put in our way there are manmade ones to contend with. Especially in the East, many rivers have all sorts of debris left over from the days of mills, dams, and logging which can pin or spear a boater. Bridge pilings are particularly likely to pin rafts or boats since they have little if any upstream water cushion.

Low-Head Dams. Low-head dams and weirs deserve special mention, since they have caused a number of drownings. They are common in the East and Midwest and appear as a uniform feature all the way across the river. They form the perfect hydraulic: they are regular, difficult to see from upstream, and almost impossible to get out of without help (see figure 1.12).

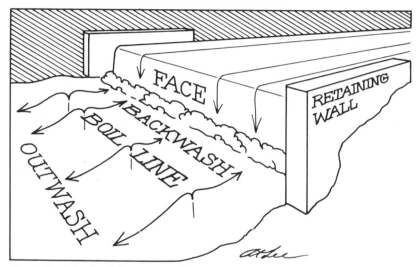

Fig. 1.12. A low-head dam.

An important feature by which to recognize a hydraulic at the base of a low-head dam is the boil line. This marks the boundary between the water flowing back upstream and the downstream flow. The water in the backwash is white, frothy, and aerated, while the water flowing downstream is darker and smooth. At the line where the two meet, the water appears to be boiling up. *Anything that gets farther upstream than the boil line will be pulled into the hydraulic by the backwash.* Rescuers must keep this in mind. Several firemen and search-and-rescue personnel who were not aware of these hazards have drowned while attempting to rescue people from hydraulics below low-head dams. One woman rescued from the backwash of a low-head dam commented that she had been through much worse-*looking* rapids. With good reason low-head dams are called "drowning machines."

This all points to the need for good educational preparation. Know what you're looking for and looking at.

Fig. 1.13. Another potentially lethal hazard is the low-head dam, which can form a regular hydraulic across the entire river. Each year there are numerous deaths in these "drowning machines." This dam is on the Oetz River in Austria.

Big/Cold Water. Even without the dangers of hydraulics and holes, big and continuous whitewater is itself a hazard for a person out of a boat or raft. Breathing, not to mention rescue, is difficult no matter how good your life jacket, and must be carefully timed. Swimming in this kind of water can lead to "flush drowning" if the swimmer aspirates enough water. Long, cold swims quickly bring on hypothermia, a lowering of the body's core temperature, which robs the swimmer of his strength, judgment, and, if prolonged, his life (see appendix I).

Combining the two is even more deadly, since an unprotected person falling into cold water (below 25 degrees Celsius) often experiences a gasping reflex, which causes him to aspirate water rapidly and drown. Glacier-fed rivers often peak during warm weather, producing a combination of warm air, which often inhibits the wearing of proper protective clothing, and big, cold water.

Rating the Rapids

Interpreting the classifications of river rapids causes a lot of confusion. The American Whitewater Affiliation (AWA) International Scale of River Difficulty grades rapids in Classes I to VI, from "easy" to "extreme risk of life."

The "Grand Canyon" system or "Deseret" scale, sometimes used in the West, rates rapids on a scale from 1 to 10. The problem with any of these scales, though, is that they attempt to define a fluid phenomenon with an arbitrary number. One person's Class III is another's Class IV. Paddlers are getting better, and by today's standards older guidebooks often overrate rapids. Nantahala Falls, for example, which used to be rated a Class V at high water, is now considered by many to be an easy Class III. Some western boaters have taken to downgrading rapids as a matter of course. A Class VI that has been successfully run becomes a Class V, and, after a few more runs, a Class IV.

Fig. 1.14. What class rapid is it? Present classification systems are vague and should be applied with caution.

The result of all this is a "system in chaos," which in some ways is worse than no system at all. Several changes, such as an open-ended decimal scale similar to that used by rock climbers or a separate letter added to the numerical classification for the danger/exposure factor, have been proposed but not adopted. Right now the only way to be sure how difficult a river is is to compare notes with other paddlers. Compare the new river to one you've already paddled: maybe it's harder than Noname Creek but easier than the Bottomdrop River. Get specifics like the gradient and volume; don't settle for vague descriptions like "It's only Class IV" or "It's easy." And no scale should be a substitute for your own judgment.

Preparation

General. Adequate, functioning equipment is critical for safety. Equipment preparation includes jobs like patching boats and repairing life jackets and helmets, tedious work best done in the off-season rather than the night before the first spring trip. It also means having the right equipment and having it *with* you.

Some paddlers go to great lengths and cost to prepare their equipment but do very little to prepare themselves either physically or mentally. Knowing your own physical abilities and limitations is important. Equally important is knowing that they change with the seasons. Boating is a seasonal sport, and after a winter's layover few of us are at the same peak of paddling ability as we were last fall. It's better to warm up on a few easy rivers than to begin pushing the limit the first day out. Your chances of injury (not to mention muscle soreness) are much less if you've maintained a regular fitness routine over the winter.

Time spent off the river can be used to expand your abilities and horizons—the middle of a rapid is not the best place to practice your strokes. If your roll is weak, get in a pool or on a lake and sharpen it up. Many clubs

Fig. 1.15. Education is an important part of paddling. Here students on the American River in California practice a strainer drill, in which a student must go from a feetfirst swimming position into a headfirst position to cross the strainer, then back again.

sponsor weekly pool rolling sessions during the winter months. Education in general is an important part of paddling. Practice and expand your paddling skills in the controlled environment of a clinic. Take a class in rescue techniques, first aid, or cardiopulmonary resuscitation (CPR) so you don't have to guess what to do in an emergency. Learn from books, magazine articles, club slide shows, outfitter's presentations, and paddling guides.

Pretrip Considerations. Before you get on the water, gather information about where you're going. A thorough knowledge of the river is essential, and a remote creek requires more research than a popular river run.

Fig. 1.16. *Check before you leave. Outfitter's shops can often provide information about the rivers you want to paddle, as well as last-minute gear and provisions.*

Consider the river. Where will you put in and take out? Are there any alternatives? How long is the run, and can it be completed in the time available? Add some extra time for lost shuttles, playing, and emergencies, and remember that the days are shorter in the spring and fall. What is the level of difficulty of the river? How much will it change if the water goes up? Where are the river gauges (and what are the safe levels?), the major rapids and hazards, and emergency evacuation access points and trails? What about the location and phone numbers of the nearest rescue squads and hospitals? Are they any landowner problems? Save yourself the pleasure of looking up the wrong end of an irate farmer's shotgun and find out before you leave. Are guidebooks or USGS topographical maps available for the river and the surrounding area?

Screen participants for paddling ability. It is much easier for a trip organizer to say no to an unqualified friend over the phone than at the water's edge, but judging paddlers you've never met or seen paddle is difficult. Ask some discreet questions (do you understand the risks? Do you know what to do in an emergency? Can you roll?). Inquire about rivers they have paddled or the names of others they have paddled with to get an idea.

Arrange for shuttles. There is no better way to get any trip off to a bad start than by a poorly organized shuttle. A botched shuttle can compromise the safety of the trip if it puts you on the river much later than expected and forces the group to bend safety rules to hurry. Some forethought about meeting locations, finding drivers, avoiding trespass on private property, and learning about road conditions will contribute to a timely start. A good map is a big help, and the mechanical condition of the shuttle vehicles must be considered. Almost everyone has a story about the shuttle that got lost, got stuck, or broke down.

Have a contingency plan. What happens if the water is too high or too low? Or if the river is dam controlled and there is no release? Can other sections of the river be run? Are there other rivers in the area of the same level of difficulty? Finding out river levels and local weather conditions is an art. Driving all night to get to a river only to find it in flood invites rash acts.

On the Water. Once at the river, get together and discuss the trip so that everyone knows what the plan is. Talk about the length of the trip and the nature of the river, and compare notes about the weather and water temperature to help determine what to wear.

Choose a leader. Paddlers tend to be independent and informal and sometimes resist this, but in the organizing stage of the trip and especially in an emergency there are good reasons for having a leader. A leaderless group may be disorganized in an emergency, and that is the very time instant action and coordination are needed. Small paddling groups (three to five people) of nearly equal ability seldom formally choose a trip leader, but in that case each individual must accept responsibility for his own actions and be prepared to assist other group members in any rescue function. In informal groups like this, individual initiative must substitute for leadership.

Designate a lead and sweep boat, so that experienced paddlers will be first and last on the river. In larger groups (ten or more boats), two or three boats can stay together as "buddy boats" the whole day. This spreads the impact of a large group over more of the river. Major rapids and a description of the takeout should be noted before starting. Times should be agreed

Fig. 1.17. Organization on the river is important. Paddlers should stay within sight of each other, and everyone should keep an eye on the boats both ahead and behind.

on, so as to keep the group moving during the day and to avoid getting caught out after dark.

Someone should be assigned to carry a first aid kit, a spare paddle, and a repair kit, and everyone should know which boats these are in. In general, the first aid kit should be carried by the most medically competent person in the group, and it should stay near the sweep boat. Groups of more than ten boaters should consider having more than one first aid kit.

Scouting

Scouting is looking before you paddle. It is the last step in preparation before actually going into a rapid. This is normally done in unfamiliar or difficult rapids, but it's always a good idea, even if you've run the rapid before. If the water has been up, for example, there might be a strainer down across the river.

When do you scout? A ledge or vertical drop will appear first as a "horizon line" across the river (see figure 1.18). The noise off the water may be louder and mist and spray apparent. Difficult rapids often appear in areas of geologic change, which you can spot by watching the shoreline. Do the contours of the land drop suddenly? Is there a staircase appearance to the boulders on shore or in the treetops? Is the river narrowing down and the banks rising? All these are invitations to scout.

Fig. 1.18. Sometimes horizon lines aren't easy to see from a boat. This one conceals a 12-foot drop on the Nantahala. Scout what you can't see.

Some people are able to scout almost everything in their boat, eddy by eddy. Most can't, and the best way is to walk. If possible, scout from both shores. You'll be amazed how the perspective changes. If possible, scout from river level: if you look down on the river from above, things flatten out and don't look as big as they really are. Obvious routes seen from on high have a way of getting lost in a confusion of waves and holes once you are on the water. Pick markers to designate your line; a particular boulder, a wave, or a landmark on shore will help define your route.

An experienced paddler will carefully study the rapids and plan the run almost stroke by stroke. However, an all too common attitude among decked-boat paddlers is "If I miss my line and flip, I'll just roll up at the bottom." Such nonchalance has gotten some people into trouble. Consider the consequences if things go wrong and have a contingency plan ready. Where are the eddies? If you end up swimming, which way will you go? How close is the next rapid?

Group scouting is usually best, because it allows for an exchange of opinions and gives the trip leader a chance to suggest tactfully that some paddlers should walk. Peer-group pressure can be a source of trouble. There is nothing wrong with running something a little over your head as long as adequate safety precautions are taken, but there are those who will encourage you to run something just to see you get hammered. If you don't feel up to it, portaging is an honorable option.

Fig. 1.19. Scout as a group. If you're not confident of your ability, portaging is an honorable option.

Leadership

Paddling is an individualist's sport, and often leadership and teamwork are purposely avoided. Yet organization, whether for a trip or for a rescue, is vital and requires leadership. This doesn't mean giving orders, except in an emergency, but designating a member of the group to give directions may make the difference between a well-organized trip or rescue and a disaster.

Fig. 1.20. Leadership on the river is critical during a rescue, because the time available is often short. Even small groups should consider designating a leader.

A good trip leader is a person with experience and river sense. He should have good judgment and good enough interpersonal skills to get along with the rest of the group, and he should be skilled on the river. "Getting along" might be the ability to organize things without appearing to give orders and to say no politely to an unqualified paddler. Good leadership may mean walking around a rapid you'd like to run yourself in order to encourage a weaker paddler not to run it, or it may mean keeping your eye on someone who has taken repeated swims and might be becoming hypothermic. It means acting as a clearinghouse of information for the other trip members and always checking everything. The trip leader is not always the strongest paddler in the group, but he should be someone with a cool head and the ability to organize and make decisions.

Saying No

We have already mentioned that you need to measure your own ability against the river. There will also be times that you'll have to measure the abilities of others, even strangers, and say yes or no to them. This requires a good eye for paddling ability and a little diplomacy. At one extreme are those who invite novices along just to see them get munched; at the other are those who refuse to let anyone but the best come because they don't want to take time out from boating for teaching or assistance.

Experts sometimes seem either to lose perspective about the skill needed to paddle difficult water, or to play it down deliberately in order to make themselves look better. This makes it hard for others to gauge such rapids objectively. Add this to the vagueness of the present rapids classification system and you have a situation in which it's easy to get in over your head. If measuring your own skills against an uncertain standard seems hard, it is even harder to measure someone else's. Ultimately the individual must determine his own qualifications, but the trip leader and the other paddlers should express candid opinions on the matter. Rather than asking whether a prospective group member can paddle Class IV water, the leader should ask what rivers he has run and at what water levels. At the put-in, some practice rolls or braces will tell the good leader more about the person's ability than will any amount of verbal description.

The "What If" Factor

Good river sense demands a special type of awareness. As you paddle you are tuned in, often on a subconscious level, to your own performance and to that of other members of the group. You are aware of the hazards of a particular rapid and are always ready to begin a rescue if necessary. Thinking like this works well when scouting rapids. As you scout, pick out the hazards and potential trouble spots. Are there ways of avoiding or minimizing the hazards? If there is a flip or a swim, what will happen? What rescues could be used? In the back of your mind you are always asking yourself "What if?"

At first you will have to think consciously about the "what if" factor, but after some practice it will become automatic. Your mind will be continually assessing potential problems, discarding some alternatives, and working out the details of others. Some may criticize this as pessimistic paddling, but by avoiding accidents and being ready for trouble we are able to be more positive about paddling in general. The test comes when something goes wrong. Time for rescue is measured in minutes and sometimes seconds. The "what if" factor may mean the difference between success and failure.

Conclusion

We close this section with an account by Charlie Walbridge of a drowning on the South Fork of the Clearwater River in Idaho (full details may be found in the *Best of the River Safety Task Force Newsletter 1976–1982)*, published by the American Canoe Association in 1983).

The kayaker in question was clearly in over his head, having lost a boat on another, easier river just two days before. He flipped, swam, and drowned in the first rapid of the run. Walbridge notes that the victim "had a tendency to 'follow' people, feeling that, in or out of his boat, he'd probably make it."

Trusting in probability is a poor substitute for good judgment and a realistic assessment of one's abilities in any case, but what about the other group members? "Many in the group felt," says Walbridge, "that someone should have said something to Chuck." There does not seem to have been a designated trip leader, but on the other hand "no one . . . expected him to attempt the river that day; he jumped in the water at the last minute." Chuck's miscalculations were his own, but other people in the group were aware of them and did not make their reservations known.

"What's that metal thing on your life jacket for?"
"I don't know, but it must be important because everyone else has one."
CONVERSATION OVERHEARD ABOUT A CARABINER,
OCOEE RIVER, JUNE 1981

· 2 ·
Equipment

On the river, proper equipment is often as important as good judgment. We have seen too many trips ruined by improper or missing equipment; inadequate equipment has also been linked to a number of accidents. Unfortunately, equipment problems can affect everyone on a trip, not just the individual paddler.

The general heading "equipment" includes personal safety gear the paddler wears; safety equipment like ropes and throw bags, which are usually carried separately; and the watercraft being paddled, whether a raft, a canoe, or a kayak. The choice of equipment is determined by the difficulty of the water, the time of year, and the location of the river. Obviously, a first descent in the Andes in spring and an afternoon float on the Buffalo River will require different equipment. But the minimum, *always,* is a life jacket for everyone and a helmet for decked boaters.

For some people, the preparation is almost as much fun as the paddling. (See, for example, figure 2.1.) We see them outfitting boats and patching gear on long winter evenings. Some are equipment freaks, who have dozens of gadgets they'll never use; there are others whose idea of getting ready for the season is to buy a new roll of duct tape (these are usually the ones who have forgotten something important, need a shuttle, and just remembered that they cracked their paddle last fall). On the river you should be able to concentrate on paddling and not have to worry about equipment failure. You must choose your own equipment, but there are some specific criteria, discussed in this chapter, that everyone should consider.

We must stress, however, that no piece of equipment, however effective, can substitute for experience, skill, and judgment. Rescue equipment can easily create more problems than it solves if it is improperly used. It is the responsibility of each individual paddler to become proficient with any equipment he or she chooses to carry.

Fig. 2.1. The well-equipped kayak. This one has a tow system installed behind the cockpit, a butane lighter and small emergency kit in a film canister in the substantial rear wall, and a throw bag clipped into the seat. A prusik loop run through the seat completes the outfitting.

Personal Safety Equipment

Life Jackets. The primary purpose of the life jacket is quite simple: to help keep your head above water so you can breathe. (We say "help" because in turbulent water no life jacket will keep your head above water all the time.) Some compromises must always be made, balancing flotation, comfort, fit, and mobility, but in general the fit and function of a life jacket are more important than arbitrary amount of flotation. Newer life jackets function more as active swimming aids rather than as passive floating assists . . .

The Coast Guard calls life jackets "personal flotation devices" (PFDs) and with typical organizational mania has classified them into Types I through V. We only need to consider Types III and V, since the others are useless for whitewater. Coast Guard–approved life jackets are required by many river management agencies, but approval is no indication of the riverworthiness of a particular life jacket, since Coast Guard testing primarily reflects off-shore ocean rescue criteria. The approval process is lengthy and expensive, and has actually inhibited life jacket design.

Type III PFDs are meant for paddlers: they are cut for comfort and mobility, and have a minimum of 15.5 pounds of flotation. The best ones are cut in vest fashion and use closed-cell foam for flotation. The amount of

Fig. 2.2. Two rescue life jackets. The HF jacket (left) has a built-in rescue belt with a quick-release buckle on the front (see figure 4.20B for rear view), while the Prijon (right) has a full harness sewn to the jacket.

flotation varies with the manufacturer, and some ("shorties") are cut very short to provide improved mobility for kayakers with a minimum of flotation. In general, the bigger the water, the more flotation you will need.

Type V is a catchall category for those PFDs that do not fit into Types I–IV. This includes PFDs designed with commercial whitewater rafting in mind. These have more flotation and a collar to help turn the unconscious wearer face up (which is fine for a lake but is of little use in whitewater). Most Type Vs are bulky and uncomfortable for paddlers to wear.

Life jackets have other benefits besides flotation. The foam will protect you if you fall while scouting, or cushion your back if you're swept into a rock either in our out of your boat. A snug, well-fitting life jacket is also warm: it provides over an inch of insulation for the critical trunk area of the body. "Shorty" life jackets don't score well in either of these areas.

None of this is going to matter if you don't have your life jacket on, whether because you didn't wear it or because it came off when you most needed it. The tattered, faded life jacket with shrunken foam is considered by some to be the emblem of the true river veteran. Forget that image and retire "ol' faithful" for safety's sake. A good test to see if the time has come is to jump in the water holding onto your life jacket so that it stays in place. If you end up floating with your nose underwater, it's time. Then try jumping in without holding onto it. If the life jacket comes up over your head, it's time for some work on the waist tie. A snug, tight fit with a sturdy waist tie is essential.

In part because of excessive regulation, U.S. life jacket design has been relatively unchanging, and the many innovative designs from European manufacturers are not available in the United States. The majority of U.S.-made life jackets are really only suitable for swimming Class III water. Most fit too loosely and have inadequate waist ties made of nylon tape that are meant to be tied with a bow knot. Some more progressive manufacturers now offer things like add-on crotch straps and heavy-duty locking waist ties. There is considerable room for improvement here, and some distributors have begun offering nonapproved (but better) life jackets and letting the paddler decide what is best.

One of the most useful features pioneered by the Europeans has been the addition of a sewn-in rescue harness (described below) or a waist belt with carabiner, sewn onto the jacket (see figure 2.3). This makes strong-swimmer rescues quick and easy and, since the harness or belt is easily released, safer.

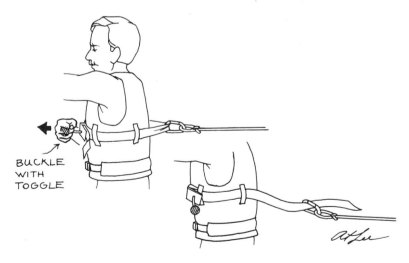

BUCKLE
WITH
TOGGLE

Fig. 2.3. A quick-release rescue harness or belt built into a life jacket allows a rescuer to get free of a tethering line in an emergency. The toggle on the release buckle is essential for finding the release in turbulent water.

This system can also be used to tie into a short belay or, in some designs, even for rappelling or vertical lowers. In the better jackets this system has been skillfully integrated into the design so that it is totally unobtrusive until needed.

Here are some suggestions for better life jacket design:

- The jacket should fit as close to the body as reasonably possible. This helps prevent it from coming off, increases insulating ability, and allows maximum freedom of movement.
- The jacket should allow maximum freedom of movement, especially around the arms and shoulders.
- A strong, locking waist tie with a quick-release is a must. Nylon tape is not acceptable.
- The jacket should provide for add-on crotch straps.
- Outside pockets for essential items, from lip balm to carabiners, should be included. One manufacturer sells a removable "Add-a-pocket" that fits over the life jacket. This also protects the life jacket from one of its biggest enemies: ultraviolet deterioration.
- The jacket should have a quick-release system for attaching a rope to the life jacket for strong-swimming rescues.

There are some ways you might want to modify your life jacket. One is to add crotch straps to keep the life jacket from coming off over your head, but this can be a bother if you have to take the jacket off and put it on a lot, and this will not always work with a sprayskirt. Another (and highly recommended) fix is to substitute a better waist tie for the standard nylon tape supplied with most life jackets. We suggest 1-inch tubular nylon webbing or a pretied prusik loop secured with a carabiner (see figure 2.4).

Rescue Harnesses. This is a chest harness that fits over the life jacket, where it may be used for a strong-swimmer rescue or to tie into a shore belay. Some models have a plastic buckle for river use and a steel buckle for "climbing" (that is, rappelling and vertical lower) applications. Some European paddlers also use them as an attachment point *for the paddler* if he is vertically pinned. They carry a small throw bag attached to the harness which, if the boat is pinned, the paddler throws out to potential rescuers. Considering that attaching a line to a vertically pinned kayak can be quite difficult, this is a sensible solution. Using a rescue harness over a life jacket is one way to add rescue capability while keeping an approved life jacket.

Fig. 2.4. This paddler wears two prusik loops girth-hitched around his waist and joined with a carabiner.

Tow Belts.   This tow system works exactly like the tow systems described later in this chapter, except that it is attached directly to the life jacket or worn as a belt over the life jacket with a quick-release around the paddler's waist and not attached to the boat. The tow is done with a short (8–10 feet) line with a carabiner on the end which fits into a small bag on the back. This is a handy system for busy instructors who switch boats often.

Helmets. These are a must for decked boaters. We recommended them on difficult rivers for rafters and canoeists too. If you use a helmet, get one worth having, (see figure 2.5). Some sold today give little more than a false sense of security. Ideally, a helmet should protect not only the top of your head but also your temples and the back of your head. Some paddlers even go so far as to use helmets with football-style face guards.

Fig. 2.5. Two types of helmet. The one on the left is fiberglass, and it gives considerably more protection than does the plastic one. (Photo: Ciro Pena/ Nantahala Outdoor Center)

Carabiners. The carabiner is a true multipurpose river tool: it can secure gear in boats, substitute for a pulley in many situations, attach haul lines to pinned boats, and do a multitude of other things. It is a good idea for everyone to carry at least one and preferably two; complicated rescues sometimes need a lot of carabiners.

There are many different kinds of carabiners. For river use, get an aluminum-alloy one—it is lighter and won't rust . . . Some carabiners have a locking device on the gate, which keeps the gate from opening at inopportune times. This is an excellent safety feature, although in the previous edition of this book we recommended against buying a carabiner with a locking gate because of the possibility of the gate's clogging with sand. Newer designs

Fig. 2.6. River carabiners. Left to right: an ordinary oval carabiner, a Chouinard 'Pearabiner" rigged with a Münter hitch, and a Chouinard "Marinabiner."

(for example, the Chouinard "Big-D" or "Marinabiner") use coarser threads that reduce the chance that this will happen. If the lock jams on a carabiner you can often release it by using a prusik loop as a strap wrench (see figure 2.7). If you don't have a locking carabiner, you can use two normal carabiners clipped in so that they open in opposite directions.

Fig. 2.7. A prusik loop can be used as a strap wrench to open a sticky carabiner lock.

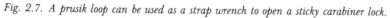
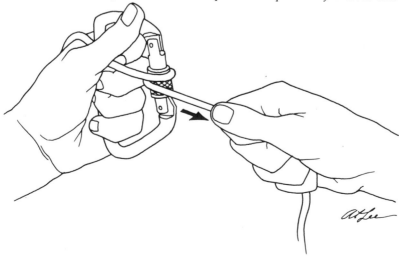

D-shaped carabiners are usually stronger than the oval ones, but probably the best all-around design is typified by the Chouinard "Pearabiner": it is a locking carabiner with a large opening that will pass a knotted ½-inch rope through. The large size and gentle radius of the opening also make it an excellent choice for a Münter hitch belay (see figure 5.22 and appendix D).

Most paddlers like to wear their carabiners on their life jackets, attached at the shoulder or the waist. However, you can injure your shoulder or collarbone if you flip over in a decked boat and the carabiner gets between you and a rock.

Descender Rings.   A descender ring can be a very handy piece of equipment for group, institutional, or outfitter use. A simple aluminum "figure 8" makes an excellent belaying tool and can also be used for rappelling.

Pulleys.   Although carabiners are often used as substitutes on the river, pulleys *do* cause less friction and so give greater pulling power to Z-drags and similar mechanical haul systems. However, they are not nearly as handy overall as carabiners and are less convenient to carry. Nevertheless, there are some excellent small pulleys available (such as those made by Rescue Systems) that paddlers might want to consider carrying (see below).

Pulley Bag.   A neat solution for the problem of carrying pulleys and keeping all your rescue gear together, the "drag bag" attaches to the rescuer's end of a throw bag rope and holds pulleys, carabiners, descender rings, prusiks, and the like. When not in use the bag fits inside the throw bag, and it comes out first in an emergency (see figure 2.8).

Fig. 2.8. The pulley bag attaches to the end of the throw bag rope and holds a number of accessories— for example, pulleys, paddle hooks, and carabiners. The pulley bag is stuffed into the mouth of the throw bag for storage, then held when the bag is thrown.

The Prusik.   A mountaineering hitch, the prusik was designed to cinch on a haul line when placed under tension. When the tension is relaxed, however, the knot can be adjusted. It is made from a loop of small-diameter rope tied together with a double fisherman's know (see appendix D). The best kind of line for this knot is a soft lay, 5–7 mm (1.4 inch–3/8 inch) kernmantle nylon rope. Outfitters catering to rock climbers stock this kind of line.

Boaters often call the loops as well as the knot a prusik. We wear two short ones girth-hitched around the waist and clipped together by a carabiner (see figure 2.4). It's an invaluable piece of equipment for quick tie-offs, anchor ties, hitching systems, and Z-drags.

Webbing and Slings.   Some paddlers prefer to substitute a soft flat or tubular nylon webbing for prusik loops. Made into slings, good-quality 1-inch climbing webbing can be used in much the same way as the prusik loops described above. Use a kleimheist knot (see appendix D) to cinch it on a rope for hauling. Webbing is generally stronger than the cord used for prusiks (typically 4,500–6,000 pounds as opposed to 1,700–2,600 pounds) and makes excellent material for anchors and sit harnesses.

Paddle Hooks.   This is another piece of gear designed for the steep rivers of the Alps. Paddle hooks come in several designs and sizes, but the most common is a small one that clamps to the edge of the paddle (see figure 2.9). The hook is clipped to a haul line; the paddle serves as an extension to place the hook on a convenient attachment point on the boat (such as the grab loop or the cockpit rim). One manufacturer makes a clamping system whereby two paddles can be joined blade-to-blade for an even longer reach.

Fig. 2.9. The paddle hook clamps to the blade of a kayak paddle and extends the paddlers reach during rescues.

Knives. These are recommended for recreational paddlers and are essential for the river professional. The right knife can also cut a boat, or cut through the floor of a broached raft to free someone. It can cut rope. Some of the haul-line systems we will describe in later chapters can develop tremendous loads when pulling on a pinned boat. If someone's arm or leg gets snarled in the line, a sharp knife will get him free. Les used his this way one day on the Nantahala when he came upon a raft towing a boy on an inner tube. When the raft hit a rock the boy was dumped into the water. When he came up, his head was caught in a noose of parachute cord. A submerged tree limb speared the inner tube and pulled the cord tight around his neck. "I leaped out of my canoe," Les remembers, "brandishing my knife like Errol Flynn. I cut the cord and swam the kid to shore. The rafters never noticed he was missing. I decided right there that my silly looking knife was worth every penny."

Get a sturdy knife with a nonrusting blade, a nonslip grip, and a positive locking sheath that can be operated with one hand. Many paddlers use folding knives, but these are hard to open with one hand. If you choose a folder get one with a locking blade. Keep your knife handy; strap or sew it to the chest, shoulder, or waist of your life jacket.

Fig. 2.10. River knives and saws. From top to bottom: ARS folding "Sierra Saw;" Stanley folding "Pocket Saw;" Gerber bolt-action "Exchange-Blade," which features an interchangeable knife and saw blade; the Gerber SST III Fieldlight; and the Gerber "Clip-Lock" River Knife

There has been a good deal of controversy about whether a knife can be used to cut through a plastic boat. It is certainly possible with the right knife. We found that a very thin, sharp blade works best; thicker blades tend to jam in the cut (for knives like this, it is essential to pull the blade at a 45-degree angle to the cut). Most of the "river knives" sold today are less than ideal for cutting boats. Their blades are too thick, and it is next to impossible to get a decent grip on their metal skeleton handles. One of the best knives we tested was a 3-ounce folding knife (the Gerber Fieldlight SST III) with a 3-inch locking blade.

We await the ideal river knife.

Saws. A lightweight folding saw can be a real help on the river. The right saw will cut through a boat or a strainer with little hesitation and is handy to have in camp. We tested a folding saw, available in almost any hardware store, that weighed only 4 1/2 ounces, takes replaceable reciprocating saw blades in various configurations, and makes short work of a plastic boat (see figure 2.10). There are a number of "camp saws" that work as well. It is certainly something a group might carry on a creek run.

Whistles. Communications can sometimes be a problem on the river because of the roar of the water. A good whistle can help. For the same reason, you should know the universal river signals (see appendix B). A whistle is also handy if someone gets lost walking out.

Fig. 2.11. Designed by one of the authors, the Kayak Rescue Kit includes a throw bag, two pulleys, a paddle hook, a Pearabiner, and a small saw; it fits (except for the saw) into the throw bag and weighs only 2 pounds, 8 ounces.

First Aid Kit. The contents of your first aid kit will vary greatly according to the location, season, duration, and anticipated difficulty of any trip. For popular rivers near well-traveled roads you need no more than a simple "ouch pouch." Extended day trips in remote locations with a group require a more comprehensive kit, one able to deal with serious lacerations, broken limbs, illnesses, and insect-sting reactions (anaphylactic shock). Wilderness expeditions require things like hypothermia thermometers and tooth-fracture treatments, as well as an array of prescription drugs available only through a doctor. (The contents of first aid kids are discussed in more detail in appendix F.)

Emergency Kit. Often carried with the first aid kit, this is intended to cope with emergencies other than physical injuries. A butane lighter or a fire-starting kit is a good idea if there is a chance you might be caught out overnight or a need to warm a hypothermia victim. You might carry an extra set of contact lenses if they are essential, or a small space blanket. Some paddlers keep items like this in a waterproof container sewn into their life jackets.

Improvised Gear. Some items must be improvised on the spot. For example, several persons have been rescued from low-head dams by fishermen who have used jumper cables from their cars.

Clothing

Proper clothing is as important as any other piece of equipment. In the past few years synthetic piles and drysuits have made substantial inroads into the wool and neoprene which have dominated the boating scene since the 1950s. Whatever you wear, the object is the same: to maintain the body's core temperature. In order to do this, certain critical areas, the trunk and head especially, must be protected against heat loss.

On the river the problem is that the paddler is constantly wet and may at any time be immersed in very cold water. The water acts in two ways: the body is wet by waves or spray, the water evaporates in the wind, and the body is rapidly chilled; or, when the body is immersed in cold water, rapid and severe heat loss by convection takes place, which leads to acute hypothermia in a very short time.

Outer Layer. The first defense is an outer layer that will protect the body from the chilling effect of the wind. Usually this consists of a paddling jacket and pants made of some kind of coated fabric to keep spray and waves off the bare skin. Both jacket and pants should be cut loosely enough to fit over the insulating layers underneath.

Insulating Layer. Wool, nylon, polypropylene pile or knits all make excellent insulators under a paddling jacket. In milder conditions they can be

Fig. 2.12. To stay warm you need at least two layers of clothing—an outer layer to cut the spray, and an inner layer of pile, wool, or neoprene. (Photo by Ciro Pena/ Nantahala Outdoor Center)

worn alone. The same layering principle applies here as in mountaineering: two or three thin layers are better than one thick one. Avoid cotton clothing.

The new synthetics are so good that they have led some paddlers to advocate eliminating wetsuits and drysuits altogether. This can be a serious mistake, however, particularly for novices, because neither synthetic materials nor wool will protect you in the water. Water will flow right through any woven fabric and directly over the skin, causing an abrupt and massive heat loss to the body. This may be an acceptable risk for experts (although the drowning of at least one expert paddler has been traced to this), but if you're still learning and expect to swim a lot, keep reading through the wetsuit and drysuit sections.

Wetsuits. Capable of replacing both the insulating layer and the outer layer, the wetsuit was developed for skin divers. Made of neoprene and coming in a variety of thicknesses and coverages, it works by letting a small amount of water in between the skin and the neoprene. The body warms

Fig. 2.13. Neoprene is still one of the best materials for extreme conditions. Wetsuits come in all shapes, sizes, and thicknesses. (Photo by Ciro Pena/Nantahala Outdoor Center)

this thin layer of water, which then acts just like any other insulating layer. If the wetsuit is fitted properly (that is, tightly) this warm water will be held against the skin even when the wearer is in the water. The neoprene will also act as a shield against waves and spray.

Against these advantages, however, it must be said that wetsuits are stiff, constricting to the active paddler, and somewhat uncomfortable. "Plumbing" arrangements are tedious for men and next to impossible for women. Wetsuits do not lend themselves well to layering, although the newer generation of thinner, more flexible wetsuits developed for surfing is much better on this count.

Drysuits. A relatively recent development in whitewater clothing is the sealed, watertight drysuit. The openings at the wrist, ankle, and neck are closed with tight-fitting latex seals. The suit is worn over normal insulating clothing. With water mostly sealed out and the body kept dry, heat loss is minimal; in fact, heat buildup is sometimes a problem. Drysuits have become very popular and have extended the paddling season for many. They are expensive, however, and require a fairly high level of maintenance, since the latex seals are easily torn, and the expensive waterproof zippers sometimes jam.

Ropes

River ropes can be divided into two main categories according to their intended use: throwing or hauling. Ropes are made either by the traditional method of twisting or braiding strands together, or by the newer technique of kernmantle construction, in which the strands are laid parallel in a core and covered with an abrasion-resistant woven sheath. Most climbing and rescue ropes are kernmantle ropes. For a simple throwing rescue, the construction (and the strength) of the rope is relatively unimportant. What is important for a throw rope is that it should float, not absorb water, and be easily handled. A certain amount of dynamic stretch is beneficial, since it will reduce the shock loading when stopping a swimmer. For most purposes a simple 3/8-inch braided polypropylene rope will suffice. However, when used for haul lines, and especially for lifelines (for example, Tyroleans), rope quality and strength become critical. For a haul or anchor line we want a rope that has a high breaking strength and that will not stretch under load. This means having a "static" (as opposed to a dynamic, or climbing, rope) kernmantle nylon rope of 1/2–5/8 inch in diameter. So far, in spite of a number of attempts, no one has come up with a rope suitable for both purposes: polypropylene throw bag rope is too weak and stretchy for serious mechanical rescues and is unsuitable for lifelines; and nylon rope absorbs water and doesn't throw well. A promising development has been the introduction of a synthetic-core 3/8-inch rope with a polypropylene kernmantle sheath, which throws and handles well but has a breaking strength of 4,500 pounds and a 1 percent stretch under load.

Throw Bags. The vast majority of throwing rescues are made with throw bags: it is a simple nylon sack stuffed (rather than coiled) with a rope and a disk of foam. It is the primary tool of rescue for the river runner, and every paddler should consider carrying one.

Throw bags typically contain about 50–70 feet of 3/8-inch polypropylene rope, with tensile strengths in the 1,700–2,000 pound range. Polypropylene rope is superior for throwing use because it does not absorb water or sink. Throw bags are easily stowed in the boat and can be quickly deployed, at least for the first throw. It does take time to restuff the bag after a throw, and second throws with loose rope are difficult. There is also a risk that the bag may become snagged, and there is no way to control the amount of rope thrown.

Throw bags come in a variety of styles and lengths (see figure 2.14). Some bags have ropes that are only 40–50 feet in length. These are very popular with kayakers because they stuff into a smaller bag than do the longer ropes and are easier to throw. Some also use smaller-diameter rope to achieve compactness, but we have found that rope smaller than 3/8-inch diameter is often weak and very hard on the hands.

Fig. 2.14. Throw bags come in many shapes and sizes. The bag at the left rear is made of nylon mesh to reduce "bucketing" and to allow easy drying.

There have been some new ideas in throw bags. One is a quick-release chest harness with a small throw bag attached to the back or side which you wear over your life jacket. If you are entrapped, you can throw the bag to rescuers and be pulled to safety. (The quick-release is there in case something goes wrong.) Another idea is to use open-weave nylon (fishnet) fabric for the bag to reduce the "bucketing" effect of the bag in the water.

Throw bag ropes are usually marginal for mechanical rescues, and neither we nor their manufacturers recommend that you use them for Tyroleans, rappelling, or similar lifelines.

Throw Ropes. Many professional river guides prefer to carry a coiled polypropylene rope rather than a bag (see figure 2.15). This is typically a stiff, twisted, 1/2-inch polypropylene rope with a breaking strength of about 1,800 pounds. A coiled rope can, with practice, be thrown as well as a bag and is quicker to retrieve for subsequent throws. For close throws, only part of the rope can be thrown, or different coils thrown to multiple victims. However, a coil of rope is much more difficult to stow than a bag and is slow to get ready for the first throw.

Fig. 2.15. An alternative to the throw bag is a coiled 60–70 foot rope of braided 1/2-inch polypropylene.

Rescue Ropes. Groups, outfitters, wilderness travelers, or those on difficult rivers where pinning is likely may opt to carry "static" nylon kernmantle ropes of 150–300 feet in length. Their breaking strengths are normally in the 8,000–10,000-pound range, making them well suited for Telfer lowers, Tyroleans, other mechanical rescues and lifeline use.

Fig. 2.16. Four types of river ropes. Top to bottom: 3/8-inch polypropylene kernmantle (breaking strength approximately 2,600 pounds), with a 5 mm nylon prusik loop attached; 3/8-inch braided polypropylene (breaking strength approximately 1,800 pounds); 1/2-inch twisted polypropylene (breaking strength approximately 1,800 pounds); and 7 mm SPECTRA (breaking strength 4,500 pounds).

Boats and Rafts

Whitewater river craft can be divided into three broad categories: rafts, open canoes, and decked boats. All have benefited over the years from improved designs and technology, and these improvements now allow us to extend the limits of the sport to ever higher levels. In extreme whitewater, however, the consequences of mistakes or equipment failure are often severe. To reduce the risks of accidents, it is important to maximize the safety features of each type of craft.

Rafts. When selecting a raft, look for multiple air chambers (four or more) and for quality materials such as neoprene, PVC, or hypalon. There should be an adequate number of D-rings attached to the sides for your purposes, and these should be large and securely attached. Hand lines along the sides should fit snugly to prevent accidental entanglement of the arms or legs.

The two most important factors in determining what class water the raft can handle are the size of the raft and the load it is carrying. Size means not only the length and width of the raft, but also the diameter of the tubes and the upturn of the ends, all of which affect the amount of water taken on. Bigger is not always better; maneuverability must be taken into account on many rivers, and although a larger raft may be slower to fill up than a smaller one, it may be so heavy when full as to be unmanageable. The maximum safe load also varies according to the class of water you expect. Do not base your calculations on the manufacturer's figures from the raft's data plate. These are for calm water *only*. A reasonable *guideline* for white-water load rating is to figure one-half the length of the raft plus the guide (for example, a 14-foot boat can carry eight people).

Two recent developments have been the self-bailing raft and the cataraft. Self-bailers have an inflatable floor laced to the thwarts, allowing the water to run out and making the raft virtually unswampable. They are also easier to unwrap because the floor does not catch the current as much as do conventional rafts. These rafts have opened up rivers previously considered commercially unrunnable. Catarafts have a frame suspended between two pontoonlike tubes. Since there is no open compartment to fill up, these boats also have no swamping worries.

Rafts must always be prepared for a flip. "Flip lines," pioneered by western rafters, are prerigged lines attached at one end to D-rings on the side of the raft or to a rowing frame. With the raft upside down, a boatman can grab the line, stand on the opposite tube, and flip the raft over in mid-current.

All too often, gear is left strewn about the raft floor, so everything should be tied or clipped securely into the raft before you start, and it should be kept that way. In an oar rig, beware of shoehorning yourself into the rowing compartment, because you will need some space if the downstream oar gets caught. In one incident, an oar was driven completely through a boatman's thigh because of a crowded rowing compartment.

On big rivers, consider outfitting rafts for double or triple rigging (see figure 2.17). When two or three rafts are tied together, the combined mass is less likely to be flipped or stopped by a hole. To prepare for this, install additional D-rings low on the tubes so that the rafts can be tied together top and bottom, which will prevent them from flipping over onto each other. The rig is controlled by sweep oars in the bow and stern.

Decked Boats. Proper outfitting of a decked boat is important for safe paddling. *Outfitting* means finishing a boat and fitting it to yourself, after you buy it but before you paddle it. Almost all boats need a certain amount of modification so that the paddler can fit snugly in the boat. The key here is to

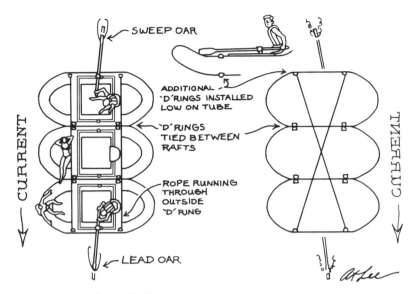

Fig. 2.17. A triple-rigged raft.

be tight enough to "wear" the boat yet not be wedged in so tightly that a quick exit is difficult.

Foam walls of some sort are an important safety item for any decked boat. Mounted vertically under the bow and stern, parallel to the length of the boat, they add deck-to-hull strength: without them the deck is likely to collapse in heavy water or in a pin. Walls are usually made from minicell, although styrofoam and ethafoam are also sometimes used. The harder the water and the more playing you do, the bigger and stronger the walls must be. Most boats have some sort of locking system for the walls to keep them upright. If not, you should secure the walls by gluing in side blocks to the deck and hull to brace the walls at the top and bottom.

Making the walls longer and thicker makes it harder to get out of the boat, particularly for long-legged paddlers, but proponents of these longer walls point out that they keep the paddler from being jammed up to his armpits in a vertical pin. On the whole, the balance of opinion seems to favor longer and thicker walls.

Many European boats, however, are designed differently, since many boatbuilders in Europe believe that the danger of a wall's falling over and entrapping a paddler's leg outweighs its benefits. Most of them (the Prijon is a good example; see figure 2.18B) have an adjustable transverse bulkhead under the deck which acts as a footbrace. This allows more room for the paddler's legs and ensures that he will not go forward if the boat hits bottom on a pin. This system has so far not found favor with U.S. manufacturers.

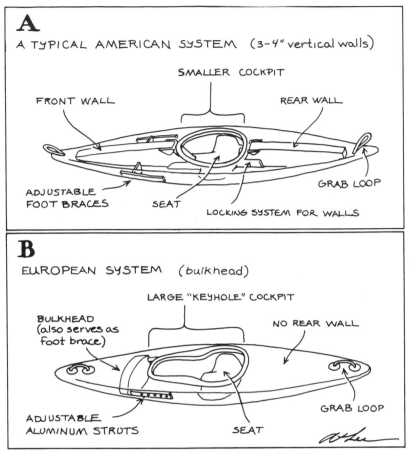

Fig. 2.18. A safely outfitted boat should have sturdy, braced walls or bulkheads to keep the deck from collapsing, strong grab loops, airbags, foot braces, and thigh braces. Most U.S. boats use the system shown in A, with vertical walls running the length of the boat, while many European boats use the system shown in B, with a keyhole cockpit and a transverse bulkhead which also serves as a footbrace.

The construction of the boat itself can have important safety implications. Fiberglass boats should have a "breakaway zone" of fiberglass without synthetic fibers around the cockpit area. The fiberglass, which is much more brittle than the tough synthetics of the hull, will fracture if the boat wraps, giving the paddler a chance to escape. This type of construction has saved several lives. Plastic kayaks are not at present made with breakaway cockpits, although at least one system (the Safety Deck) has demonstrated promise (see figure 2.19). Many U.S. boatbuilders are, however, realizing the safety value of larger cockpits, something else that has been a feature of European boats for some time. A large cockpit is cheaper and easier to manufacture than a breakaway one, although some paddlers complain that the larger area of the sprayskirt makes it more prone to blow off in big water. One possible compromise solution is the "keyhole" cockpit: a long, narrow, cockpit in which the paddler can raise his knees (see figure 2.20).

Fig. 2.19. *The U.S.-designed Safety Deck shows considerable promise for reducing paddler entrapment in kayaks. It is an alternative to a large cockpit, but is more expensive to manufacture. (Photo courtesy Outdoor Safety Systems)*

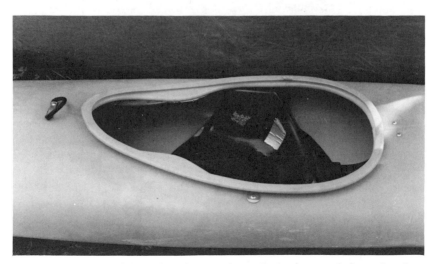

Fig. 2.20. *The "keyhole" cockpit, long popular in Europe, has recently been adopted by Infinity, a U.S. manufacturer. Note also the "broach loop" in front of the cockpit.*

Older plastic boats often get softer with age, making them more likely to deform and "stick" on an obstacle. It may be that plastic boats are more dangerous than fiberglass ones, but since most recreational boats are now made of plastic, the question is moot.

While on the subject of design, a word about Squirt boats is appropriate. These small stunt kayaks have attracted a growing following, especially in the East. Squirt boats require constant expert attention and are tiring to paddle, especially in cold water, since the paddler is usually in it up to his armpits. These boats dive like submarines and some of the accepted maneuvers, like mystery moves and pillow squirts, invite pinning or broaching. They have been involved in a number of accidents. We do not pass judgment on any paddler's choice of boats, but the dangers of these little craft are not to be taken lightly.

Another important safety item is the grab loop. Grab loops should be securely attached at bow and stern and made of at least 8-mm rope, because if you are vertically pinned one of them is going to be the most convenient handle. Many boats sold today, unfortunately, have inadequate grab loops. Some boaters attach a third grab loop, or "Blackadar handle" just behind the cockpit to give a swimmer something to hang on to in big water. Another recent innovation is the "broach loop" (see figure 2.20), a steel ring or nylon loop mounted in front of the cockpit. This has yet to be thoroughly tested, but at the very least, it offers another point of attachment for a pinned boat, and in the best of circumstances may allow a haul line to pull the front deck up enough to free an entrapped paddler.

Another useful features to add is a towing system for getting swamped boats back to the shore (see figures 2.21 and 2.22). Most paddlers rely on the "bulldozer" method: putting their bow in the cockpit of the swamped boat and pushing it to shore. A more efficient way is to use a towing system that puts you in the normal ferry position upstream of the swamped craft. The center-mounted system (just aft of the cockpit) allows the tow boat to swivel and therefore control the ferry angle more precisely. Systems that tow the boat near the grab loop make ferrying more difficult, since the towed boat tends to pull the towing boat around to face upstream. Any tow system should have a foolproof release system, unless you like the idea of having a 1,000-pound anchor permanently attached to your boat. One German tow system attaches to the hull with a plastic through-bolt that will break under pressure, even if the paddler is unable to release it. Be sure to test the release on any tow system before you use it.

Any of the several tow systems shown here (see figure 2.23) will work well. Most are inexpensive and easy to install. They use the jam cleat, a standard sailing item available through most marine hardware stores, to make a quick-release system. You can now buy preassembled towing kits, from simple ones that use the jam cleat to the more expensive German items.

Fig. 2.21. A & B. Two types of tow system. The cam cleat system (see figures 21A and 22A) is simple and inexpensive. The German HF Kayak system (see figures 21B and 22B) tows with a quick-release buckle near the cockpit, attached to the boat with a plastic through-bolt. The bolt is designed to break even if the paddler is unable to reach the buckle. Having the towing attachment pivot near the cockpit makes holding a ferry angle easier.

Fig. 2.22A. An installed tow system. It can be used for towing boats, carrying retrieved paddles, and ferrying lines.

Fig. 2.22B. The HF system.

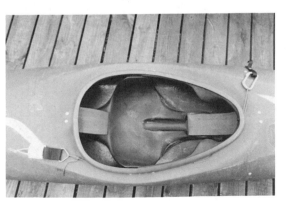

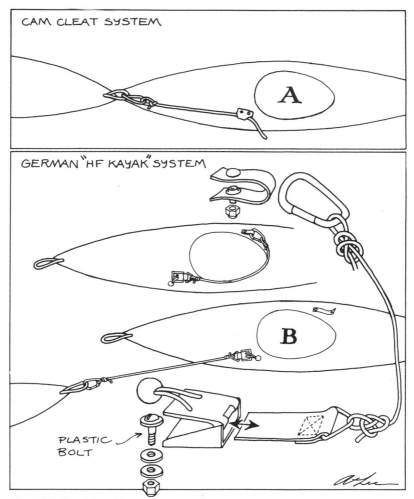

Fig. 2.23. Two types of tow system.

Open Canoes. The new generation of ABS designs has allowed open canoes to run water once reserved for decked boats. Even the Niagara Gorge has been run in an open canoe.

Some people choose the open canoe because of the reduced risk of entrapment. Walls are not necessary, as they are in decked boats, but a fitted foam block or "horse" placed under the thwarts (see figure 2.24) will go far toward eliminating the danger of a canoe pin or paddler entrapment. Blocks are bulky, which leads some people to prefer airbags, but although airbags will displace water and make the boat easier to swim to shore they do not

Fig. 2.24. This canoe has a fitted styrofoam block in the center. It takes up room but makes the canoe less vulnerable to pinning.

add any structural strength. Commercially available molded plastic "saddles" serve much the same purpose. Another system of flotation, popular in New England, involves attaching a 4-inch-thick layer of ethafoam to both sides of the hull of the canoe, which gives more room to carry duffel.

Canoeists often install thigh straps or braces to improve their control over the boat. Straps should have a quick-release and be made of a wide, stiff material that won't snag the paddler in a wet exit. Position them so that they don't come up around your groin but fit lower down, toward your knees. Velcro makes an excellent strap fastener, since unlike a buckle it will release under strong pressure. For an example of what can happen with sticky straps, see the end of chapter 7.

Unless you line your canoe a lot, there is little reason to use painters over 8 feet long. The loose painter becomes a hazard in an upset and may snarl the paddler. Store it under shock cord when it is not in use. If you have aluminum gunnels, go over them periodically with a file and remove any sharp edges. We don't recommend wooden gunnels or thwarts for serious whitewater. They can be a hazard if they break into spearlike splinters when the boat pins. A spare paddle is a good idea, but make sure the hold-down system works: you should be able to get the paddle easily, but have it secure if the boat overturns.

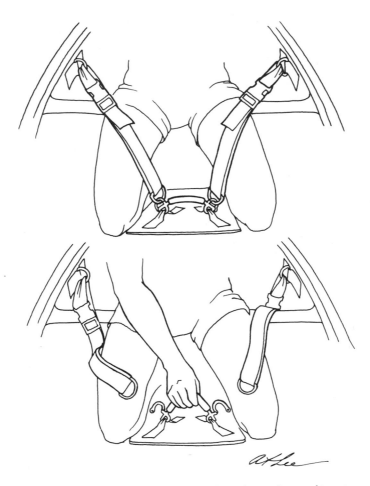

Fig. 2.25. Thigh straps are an integral part of the outfitting of most whitewater canoes. They should allow the paddler to exit without entanglement. This design quick-releases when the paddler pulls the handle in the center. In order to avoid the type of entanglement described at the end of chapter 7, both straps should have a quick release.

Conclusion

Many safety decisions are best left to the individual. Others, such as the need for decked boaters to wear life jackets and helmets in good condition, should be universally recognized. A river-guide friend of ours is an expert paddler with many first descents (including Niagara Gorge) to his credit, but he used to be a real cheapskate when it came to personal gear. His life jacket had long ago lost its waist tie, and his helmet was carved out to fit his huge head. While guiding on the Ocoee one day he was flipped backward out of his raft and hit his head. "I was helpless," he said later. "I was a competitive swimmer in college, but there I was floating face down, unable to take a stroke." Fortunately, another raft was able to get to him before things got worse, and the first thing he did after getting out of the hospital was to buy a new life jacket.

Some decisions, such as whether to wear a knife or install a towing system, should be determined by the difficulty of the water and your personal preferences. There is a definite attraction to paddling with a minimum amount of gear, and each of us must balance the rewards against the consequences.

Fig. 3.1 For decked boaters the quickest means of self-rescue is the Eskimo roll, but it must be practiced to be effective.

· 3 ·
Self-Rescue

R ivers keep flowing, regardless of our personal misfortunes. An important lesson for all paddlers to learn from this is that you have to take
care of yourself on the river. Charlie Walbridge, of the American Canoe
Association River Safety Task Force, says that most of the recreational paddlers who drowned in American rivers in 1983 were not entrapped and were
wearing life jackets. They perished floating through whitewater, unable to
get to shore.

In chapter 1 we saw the importance of preparation, both mental and
physical, and of good judgment. We also discussed some of the leader's
responsibilities for the safety of the group and the individual. In this chapter
we'll concentrate on the individual paddler and on how he can deal on his
own behalf with some of the hazards we've defined.

We recommend that you don't paddle alone, but even in a group the
responsibility for your own safety rests in large part with you. You are the
one who wanted to paddle, and you are the one who must ultimately take
the blame for your miscalculations. It follows that you should be able to
rescue yourself.

For those in decked boats, the quickest and most obvious means of self-
rescue is the Eskimo roll. It is the best insurance policy you can invest in,
and like any other aspect of the sport it requires practice. A good roll is a
real boost to your self-confidence, which in turn reduces the likelihood of
more serious mistakes. Nevertheless, there is also a time to swim. Overconfi-
dence and misplaced pride ("I never come out of my boat") are as bad as
too little confidence. In open water it is all right to keep trying to roll, and if
you scouted thoroughly you should know when you turn over whether a
hazard is coming up. Often it's a matter of experience: novices tend to bail
out too soon and experts to stay in too long. Experience will give you almost
a sixth sense for where you are in a rapid when you find yourself upside
down.

Although the number of open canoeists who have a roll is increasing, most must still rely on the swimming technique of self-rescue. When that last low brace fails and you capsize, get to the upstream side of the boat when you come up. If things look bad, abandon the boat and swim for shore. If it seems safe to do so, work your way to the upstream end of the boat, grab the painter (but don't wrap it around your arm), and swim the boat to shore. Sometimes it is possible to right a swamped boat and paddle it to shore.

Rafters can also use self-rescue after a flip. If the raft is equipped with flip lines (as described in chapter 2), it can often be righted while in the water (see figures 3.2 and 3.3). If the raft can't be righted, the rafters should attempt to climb on top of the capsized raft and paddle it to shore, after first checking to see what it downstream (figure 3.4). Another method is to have a line or throw bag rigged so that a crew member can grab it, swim to shore, and pendulum the raft in (figures 3.5 and 3.6). If this is not possible, the crew should try to swim the raft to shore by holding on to the D-rings or painters.

Swimming with a boat or raft can be more dangerous than swimming without one, especially on rocky rivers, where there is a chance of getting squashed between the boat and a rock. In big water the extra buoyancy of your boat is an asset, but stay on the upstream side. Wide, cold rivers, such as those in Canada and Alaska, present another problem. Although the whitewater may not be difficult, a swimmer may die of hypothermia before reaching shore. With a swamped decked boat a paddler can sometimes

Fig. 3.2. The prepackaged flip line is a new development in rafting self-rescue. It stows neatly out of the way, but after a flip . . .

Fig. 3.3. . . . it can be used to right the raft as shown.

reduce his exposure by crawling on top of the boat and paddling it like a surfboard. Pairs of open-canoe paddlers in this situation can try a flatwater technique: the Capistrano flip (see figure 3.7). This is accomplished by getting under an upside-down canoe, and doing a scissors kick and flipping the boat at the same time. Both canoeists then grab the gunnels, and while one holds on, the other slides into the canoe with a scissors kick. This usually cannot be done if there is duffel in the canoe.

Fig. 3.4. Another method of self-rescue for the rafter is to get up on the upside-down raft and paddle it to shore. Obviously this only works in fairly calm water.

Fig. 3.5. Yet another method of rafting self-rescue. A throw bag is tied and clipped into the bow D-ring of the raft . . .

Fig. 3.6. . . . and the rafter unclips the bag after the flip, swims to an eddy, and pendulums the raft in.

Fig. 3.7. Though not normally considered a method of whitewater self-rescue, the Capistrano flip can be used by canoeists on wide, cold rivers where the whitewater is not too severe.

It's always a good idea, if you can, to hang on to your equipment if you have to swim. However, bear in mind that equipment is cheap and lives are not. This may sound obvious, at least one paddler drowned on the Chattooga because she chose to hang on to her boat rather than to throw a rope and was entrapped in the Chattooga's infamous Left Crack.

We recommend that every paddler swim a "safe" rapid at least once a season to renew his respect for the force of the water and to keep in practice if his roll fails. Novices and experts alike should do this. Charlie Walbridge notes in the *Best of the River Safety Task Force Newsletter* that "many experts make lousy victims." Often the transition from hero paddler to helpless victim is a hard one, and one reason for this is that paddlers seldom practice swimming.

On shallow, rocky rivers the standard defensive position for swimming in a rapid is lying on your back with your feet downstream (see figure 3.8). Try to maintain a horizontal position as near to the surface as possible, always looking downstream and preparing to fend yourself off rocks with your feet. Don't float passively from one rapid to the next: kick with your legs and backstroke with your arms. A sidestroke works well in deeper water or when extra power is needed, such as when crossing an eddy line. Swim aggressively: boating techniques like ferries and eddy turns can be used out of the boat as well as in it to help you move toward the shore (see figure 3.9).

Swimming in big, deep water on wider rivers, where the danger of foot entrapment is minimal, requires a different technique (see figure 3.10). In big waves you must time your breathing for the troughs of the waves. A crawl stroke on your front will work better than swimming on your back, but here again you should use applicable boating techniques to control your progress. Especially in cold or difficult water, head for shore as fast as possible. Rescue yourself: *never assume someone else will do it.*

Fig. 3.8. *Defensive swimming in shallow water.*

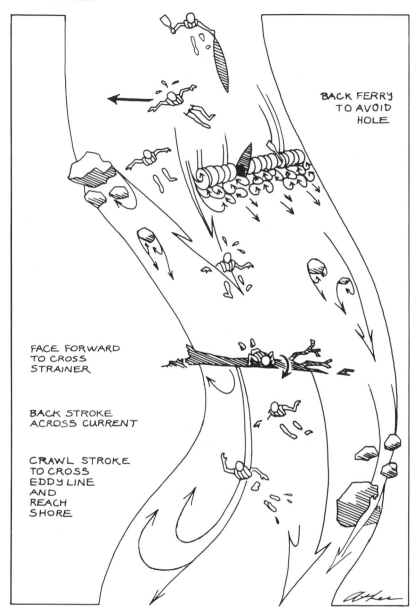

BACK FERRY
TO AVOID
HOLE

FACE FORWARD
TO CROSS
STRAINER

BACK STROKE
ACROSS CURRENT

CRAWL STROKE
TO CROSS
EDDY LINE
AND
REACH
SHORE

Fig. 3.9. Swim aggressively, using techniques like ferries and eddy turns to move across the river to safety. Here a swimmer ferries across the main current toward the eddy line, crosses a strainer, then breaks through the eddy fence with a crawl stroke.

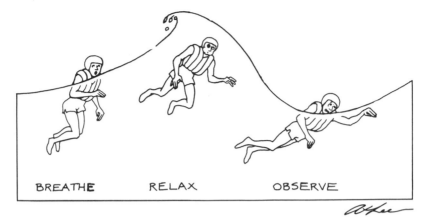

BREATHE   RELAX   OBSERVE

Fig. 3.10. Swimming in big, deep, water requires timing your breathing for the troughs of the waves. Since the danger of foot entrapment is minimal, a crawl stroke may be the best option for getting ashore quickly.

Fig. 3.11. Two canoeists swimming in whitewater. They are upstream of the boat, facing downstream with their feet up and in front of them.

Strainers

If you find yourself swept unavoidably toward a tree-choked strainer you should change your position from feetfirst to headfirst (see figure 3.12). A feetfirst position will tend to make you wash under the trunk or limbs, which is the last thing you want. Try to swim faster than the current, using a crawl stroke, and look at the tree. Is the trunk slippery? Are there limbs you can grab? You must try to get *up* on the tree and out of the current. As you hit the tree, let the force of the current assist you in keeping your momentum up as you crawl onto it. If your boat is floating with you, don't let it block your movements or pin you against the tree.

A last resort if you can't get up on the tree, whether because the current is too fast or the trunk too large, plan to dive underneath it, head first. Time your breathing and plan on pulling yourself through the branches. Don't let your body get parallel to the main trunk.

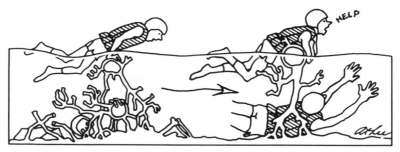

Fig. 3.12. Strainers.

Entrapment

From the self-rescue standpoint the best way to deal with entrapment is to avoid it. This means not trying to walk in water deeper than your knees and swimming with your feet up and in front of you when in shallow water. Once an entrapment occurs, it is difficult, if not impossible, for the victim to escape unaided. It is hard to stand if your foot gets caught, and if your whole body is immersed, the force of the water will be more than twice as great as on the entrapped limb (see appendix C). If you are entrapped, though, you may be able to gain valuable rescue time if you can push yourself off the bottom and dog paddle with your hands. If the water is not too swift, you may be able to get an occasional breath and survive until someone can reach you. In one such situation a man survived for over two hours until he was rescued.

Broaches, pins, and boat entrapments will be covered in more detail in chapter 6, but here we'll consider some things a paddler can do to help himself in these situations. A boat is broached when it is pushed sideways onto a solid object by the current and held there. The danger of broaching is that the boat may collapse and entrap the paddler.

In a broach, the severity of the situation depends on the position of the boat and the amount of water pushing on it. Only experience can give you a real appreciation of this, but if the water pressure is great enough to blow your sprayskirt off the cockpit rim, you are in dire danger of wrapping the boat, and it's time to get out in a hurry. You may have a chance to lean into the rock and push yourself off it with your hands. Sometimes you can push off with your paddle or shift your weight so that boat moves, but remember that the boat may wrap at any time: you must be prepared to get out as quickly as possible. The more doubtful you feel about the situation, the less time you should spend trying to get the boat off. A quick exit is usually the best choice; but remember, though, that the same rocks that pinned the boat may entrap you also.

Holes

Paddlers in decked boats surf holes to practice balancing in the hole and then paddling out. They enjoy doing this, but they also know that sometime in the future they will find themselves in a hole by accident and may need those escape skills. Before surfing an unknown hole, look at it carefully. Is water flowing out of the sides? Is there a weak spot in the backwash to escape through? Consider also what is downstream if you have to swim out. Some paddlers experiment by sending in a friend first ("Sure, it's okay. Surfed it last week. Go ahead while I adjust my sprayskirt."). This method has its adherents, but it doesn't win friends.

Fig. 3.13. Paddlers in decked boats often surf holes to practice balancing in the hole and then paddling out.

In a decked boat the best system of self-rescue in a hole is to paddle out. Try different directions: some sections of the backwash may be weaker than others. Paddle forward and backward, and try drawing downstream. Stroke on both sides in a kayak, not just on the downstream bracing blade. Canoeists should be able to switch and brace on either side. If paddling fails, turning over in the hole and extending the paddle will sometimes allow the downstream current beneath the backwash to catch your body and the paddle and pull you out. As a last resort, pop the spray skirt and hope the less buoyant boat will wash out with you still in it. Keep trying to get out, but don't make the mistake of letting yourself become exhausted. In a violent hole it takes a lot of effort to stay in control: if you can't get out, swim for it early. The best escape is to flip upside down and dive down under the backwash.

An open canoe caught in a hydraulic will amost always swamp quickly, which may cause it to wash out. But be careful: being in a large hydraulic with an open canoe can be dangerous if you and it are trading places.

If caught in a hole, rafters should quickly move to the downstream side of the raft to keep it from flipping (see figure 3.14). Sometimes the raft will fill with water and flush out on its own. Sometimes it can be paddled out or roped out from shore, but a raft full of water is *heavy* and may have a will of its own. You may have to swim out and leave the raft in the hole, especially if there is a risk of hypothermia. Get out by diving out over the backwash of the hole from the downstream tube of the raft.

It is very dangerous, if the raft is caught in a hydraulic, for a crew member to end up underneath it. The swimmer will be recirculated in the usual

Fig. 3.14. A raft caught in a large hole. If the raft flips or someone falls out, a swimmer may get trapped underneath the raft. These rafters have moved to the downstream side of the raft to keep it from flipping, while a shore-based rescue party attempts to pull the raft out with a rope.

way but will not be able to breathe if he comes up under the raft. Sometimes swimmers in this situation can be reached by hanging over the downstream tube and feeling under the raft.

Low-head dams form a hazard from which escape by self-rescue is very difficult. A swimmer will surface at the boil line only to find himself sucked back into the water pouring over the dam. The water will then force him down to the bottom and then up again at the boil line, and then the whole frightening process will start over again. To complicate matters, some dams have exposed reinforcing bars of steel, which can entrap or skewer a swimmer. Debris floating around in hydraulics (logs, for example) can hit a swimmer, though you can sometimes hang on to a piece of debris for additional flotation. If you are caught in a low-head dam, try to take guarded breaths and stay relaxed (see figure 3.15). Save your strength: you can't fight the water. Try to work your way toward the shore while being recirculated. More often than not there will be sheer concrete retaining walls buttressing the sides of the dam, but you may be rescued from the sides if someone can reach you. Sometimes, in smaller hydraulics, it is possible to swim out by diving down and catching the underlying jet of water as you are being recirculated. Otherwise, try to swim downstream only at the area of the boil line, preferably just before you surface. *Do not take off your life jacket* in an attempt to swim out of the hydraulic: if you fail you will be in much worse shape than before.

Sometimes you have to use your imagination. One fireman got out of a low-head dam by dragging himself along the bottom of the river, clinging to exposed reinforcing bars and rocks.

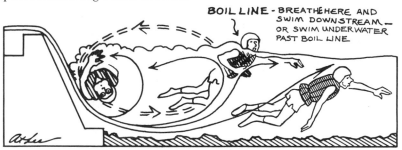

BOIL LINE - BREATHE HERE AND SWIM DOWNSTREAM — OR SWIM UNDERWATER PAST BOIL LINE

Fig. 3.15. Self-rescue in a low-head dam.

Conclusion

Not all methods of self-rescue will be found in a book. A friend of ours found himself trapped in his boat at the bottom of a drop on Alabama's Little River. He is a big, strong guy, and rather than drown he began tearing the cockpit out of his fiberglass kayak with his hands. The boat was a commercial model with a breakaway cockpit, and he was able to break enough of it away to get his legs out and swim free. If it's life or death, almost no method is too extreme.

Fig. 4.1. The basic body belay. This rope thrower is ready to belay when the rope comes taut. He should be wearing a life jacket.

· 4 ·
Rescue by Rope

The most useful single tool in any rescue, from the simple capsize to the most complicated Tyrolean rescue, is the safety rope. In chapter 2 we examined the types of ropes available. The choice is up to the user, but every whitewater paddler should consider carrying a rope and know how to use it. In this chapter we will cover the uses and techniques of rope rescue and will use the term *rope* generically.

The Throwing Rescue

Most rope rescues are made with a rescuer standing on the shore, throwing a rope to a victim, and hauling him in (see figure 4.1). It sounds simple, but few people can accurately throw a rope—rope throwing requires practice. The goal of a good throw is pinpoint accuracy at the rope's full extension. The position of the safety rope is the first consideration. A common mistake is to stand directly opposite the most likely point of capsize in an effort to get closer to a potential accident. The best place is usually farther downstream, because it takes time for the paddler to surface and to look at the rope thrower before the rope is thrown (see figure 4.2). How far downstream you position yourself will depend on such factors as the speed of the current, the distance of the next rapid, how many roll attempts may be made in a decked boat, and the presence of eddies to swing the swimmer into. Remember: if you are too far upstream and miss, you may have a hard time getting back down along the riverbank. It's often better to be a bit too far downstream.

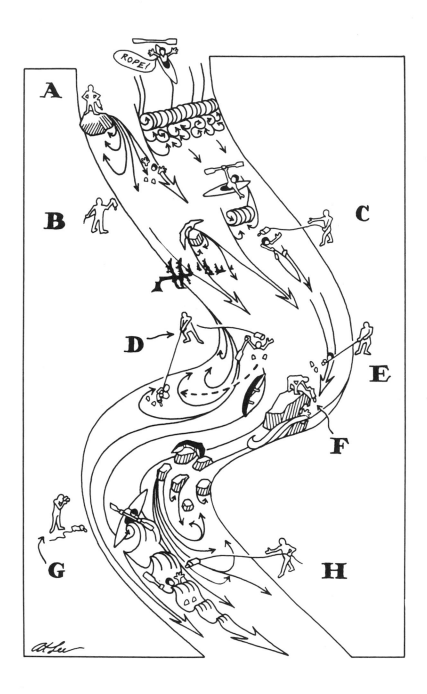

In long or hazardous sections of whitewater, you may need several rope throwers. If possible, they should be positioned above or opposite hazards like large keeper hydraulics and undercut rocks. In sections of continuous whitewater, finding a pool or eddy for rescue may be a problem.

The thrower must also consider what to do when the victim has got hold of the rope. The current will usually swing him in to shore like a pendulum. Position yourself so that the swimmer doesn't swing into a greater hazard or get caught in the full current. Look for an eddy to land your catch in. This may require you to move after the throw has been made, so check your route before you throw. Many rope rescues have failed because the rescuer had lead feet.

Before throwing, always try to get the attention of the swimmer. Yelling or whistling will usually get him facing the right way, but it is better to establish eye contact. Once the rope is in the water it is hard for the swimmer to see it. Even though the rope floats, currents will often suck it beneath the surface. Some people, especially those new to the river, will become very disoriented while swimming a rapid and will not respond to you. If you can't communicate before throwing, you must actually try to hit the swimmer with the rope (usually in the head) to get his attention. Be careful with this technique if you are using a water-filled throw bag on a subsequent throw.

In the excitement of a rescue the throw is often made too soon—while the swimmer is still upstream of the rope thrower's position. This increases the distance the rope must be thrown and so usually decreases the accuracy of the throw. The throw should be timed so that the swimmer is at the minimum possible distance from the thrower.

If you miss it is better to err slightly to the *upstream* side of the siwmmer. The rope will float faster on the surface of the water than will a swimmer who is backstroking against the current with his feet pointing downstream, and the rope is likely to drift into the swimmer without requiring that he

Fig. 4.2. Setting rope: Position A gives good visibility and has an eddy behind, but is of little use to a swimmer or an upside-down boat in the fast water of the chute; B is a better place to pick up swimmers coming out of the chute or hydraulic, but the rope thrower must get them in before the strainer downstream; C is set close enough to a hole to rescue a swimmeer either in or below it. Both C and D are set to swing a swimmer into a convenient eddy; E is set to catch a swimmer who might go into an undercut; F is too close to the undercut for a rope throw, but this would be an effective rescue position if a paddler were trapped there; at G, would-be rescuers must be ready to throw. This rescuer is too close to the hazard and would not be able to hit a swimmer washing out of the hole or a decked boat after several roll attempts; H is a better position: below the hazard with an eddy nearby.

compromise the defensive swimming position. If the rope is downstream of the swimmer, he will have to swim headfirst to retrieve it.

Ideally, the rope thrower should stand somewhat above the level of the river. Standing on a boulder or up on the bank a bit gives better visibility and allows more time for the rope to pay out while in the air, but too much height will reduce the working length of the rope and increase the time you must allow for it to reach a swimmer who may be moving downstream very quickly. For most situations the optimum height is about 4–6 feet above the river.

Never tie off the rope when throwing to a swimmer: the rope may become entangled around a part of his body, even his neck, and you may need to let go of the rope to release the tension. If you think it may be difficult to hold the rope, use the belaying technique instead. Pass the rope around a tree, a boulder, or your own body to increase the friction on it and give it extra hold power (see figures 4.3 and 4.4). If you have a rescue harness, either sewn onto or worn over a life jacket, you can use that for belaying by tying it to an anchor sling around a tree or boulder. Belaying is more effective than simply holding the rope in your hands and much safer than tying it off.

Belays may be either dynamic or static. In a static belay, the rescuer throws the rope, assumes the belay position, and "puts the brakes on." The disadvantage of this technique is that when the rope suddenly becomes taut the impact may be too great and either the swimmer may lose his grip on the rope or the rescuer may be pulled in. The dynamic belay (see figure 4.5), which brings the swimmer to a more gradual halt, is usually better. The rescuer moves downstream with the swimmer while swinging him in to shore. This reduces the loading shock on the swimmer. Another form of

Fig. 4.3. This rope thrower has the rope wrapped around her body in simple body belay. She is near enough to a tree to be able to wrap the rope around it to increase friction if the body belay isn't enough.

Fig. 4.4. The friction belay uses something like a tree or boulder to increase friction. The rope can be released if need be.

Fig. 4.5. The dynamic belay. The rope thrower runs down along the bank to decrease the loading shock on the swimmer. The banks must be fairly open for this technique to be used.

dynamic belay is to let the excess rope run through your hands, then gradually tighten your grip on the rope to reduce the braking impact on the swimmer. The rope should be run over your life jacket, and you must carefully watch the speed of the rope to avoid burns. A long throw will not usually allow enough excess rope for this technique. Dynamic belaying is also a useful technique when there is no nearby eddy and the rescuer must follow the swimmer.

Swimmers should go for the rope aggressively. (Remember self-rescue? Help yourself!) When you get to it, hold the rope to your chest with your feet downstream. Face upward and do not look at the rescuer: turning over and facing toward the rope may cause you to dive. Never wrap the rope around any part of your body (except in cold water when the hands may not be functioning well, the rope may be clamped under the armpits and then held against the chest). In the proper position the victim will plane on the water, and a breathing pocket will form immediately downstream (see figure 4.6A and B).

In extremely fast water the air pocket may be lost. If the swimmer holds the rope with one hand over his head and the other on his chest, his body will plane better, and he will be able to breathe more easily. It is harder to hold the rope this way, however, than with two hands across the chest (see figure 4.6C).

Throwing Techniques

There are three primary methods of throwing a rope or bag: underhand, overhand, and sidearm. Each can be effective, but no matter which style you use it is important to throw with your whole body and not just with your arm. Watch javelin or discus throwers: they use their whole bodies, hurling from the legs through the upper torso and following through with the arm. To get the full extension of the rope you must do the same.

Most people stand with their bodies facing upstream. To make use of your full power potential, however, you should stand sideways, with your throwing arm on the side away from the river. If you are right-handed and are standing on river right (that is, on the right bank as you face downstream), this means your body will be facing downstream and you will be looking upstream over your left shoulder (see figure 4.7).

Before throwing, look for obstacles:. slalom-gate wires, bystanders, or tree branches. If you are using a throw bag, loosen the cord lock but do not open it to the widest position. Opening it all the way will cause a "bucketing" effect as water flows into the mouth of the bag. When throwing a coiled rope, split the coils of the rope between your throwing hand and your

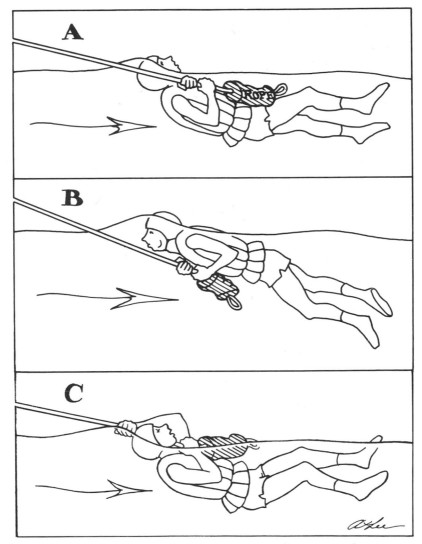

Fig.4.6. (A) The right way to hold a rope in whitewater. The rope is over the shoulder and held close to the chest, with the swimmer facing up and away from the rope thrower. The swimmer tends to plane to the surface and the water forms an air pocket around his face. (B) The wrong way. The swimmer, lying on his belly and looking at the rope thrower, gets a faceful of water. His body may even tend to dive—the last thing he wants.(C) In very swift water, the swimmer may want to hold his arm above his head, which will cause his body to plane better.

Fig. 4.7. The correct throwing position for a right-handed thrower—facing slightly downstream, looking over the shoulder.

Fig. 4.8. The coiled rope is split into two coils and thrown as shown.

Fig. 4.9. The same principle is applied to the throw bag, after the initial throw. This saves time because you don't have to stuff the bag if repeated throws are necessary.

holding hand. The loops of rope must be evenly sized and not tangled. If possible, take one or two practice throws to help judge the current and to work the kinks out of the rope.

It may seem unnecessary to add that the thrower should hang onto the rope, but many times we have seen even the professionals throw the whole rope away. Be sure you have a good grip on the end before you let fly.

Underhand. This is the most popular and perhaps the most natural-feeling throw. The thrower swings the rope back and forth a few times to develop a rhythm and then releases it (see figures 4.10 and 4.11). The release should be at about a 45-degree angle to the surface of the water: a premature release will make the rope hit the water only a few feet in front of the thrower; a late release will make the rope go straight up and then down on the head of the would-be rescuer (much to the amusement of everyone but the swimmer). The underhand is best used for close throws. It can be difficult in brushy or otherwise restricted areas.

Sidearm. Many people, especially smaller ones, find they can improve their distance with the sidearm throw, but this gain often comes at the expense of accuracy. The side arm motion, similar to that used by the discus thrower, makes it easier to use your whole body. It also requires a fair amount of clear space in which to throw.

Figs. 4.10. Position for the underhand throw.

Fig. 4.11. The underhand throw.

Overhand. The overhand throw is superior to the other techniques in many ways. Whereas the other methods need some preparation, the overhand throw can be used on the run with little preparation (a rescuer can run into a throw, like a baseball player). It requires less room in which to throw and can be used on brushy banks, over the heads of a raft crew, and in waist-deep water. The rope can also be thrown with greater velocity over greater distances. This technique usually works better with a smaller throw bag (see figures 4.12 and 4.13).

Multiple Swimmers

A rescuer is sometimes faced with a situation involving multiple swimmers—when a raft overturns, for example. If the swimmers are bunched closely together, throw the rope to the middle of the group. If they are separated, throw to the ones farthest away but still within reach of the rope. With luck, some of the others can grab the rope too. If you have a coiled throw rope split into two coils as described earlier, you can throw one coil to one nearby swimmer and the other coil to the next. Be sure to hang on to the middle of the rope (see figure 1.2 for an example).

Bear in mind that a single rescuer will have a hard time holding more than two swimmers with a static belay unless he is able to use a fixed object like a tree. In that case, use a dynamic belay, which can handle a surprisingly large load.

Multiple swimmers should all hold on to the rope rather than each other.

Figs. 4.12. Position for the overhand throw.   *Fig. 4.13. The overhand throw.*

Tag Line Rescues

Unlike throwing rescues, which are intended for moving swimmers. tag line rescues are used to aid a victim who is involuntarily fixed in one position—for example, in some cases of foot entrapment or boat pinning, or for a person held in a keeper hydraulic.

A tag line is simply a line stretched across a river and brought to the level of a stationary victim. A floating tag line has some sort of flotation device attached to it to keep the rope on the surface of the water and to provide something for the victim to hang on to. A snag tag, on the other hand, is a bare or weighted line used to snag fully or partly submerged objects.

Tag line rescues require planning and team effort but have the advantage of being relatively uncomplicated. As a shore-based rescue, they are safe for rescuers.They can be set up quickly, and untrained spectators can often be used to manage the ropes from shore.

Rope Ferries. The first step in setting up a tag line, as well as in many other river rescues, is to get a rope across the river. This often isn't as simple as it sounds. On a narrow river or creek you can simply throw or swim the rope across, but for wider rivers you will have to ferry it across, using whatever craft is available. Before beginning the ferry, coil the rope neatly on the shore to reduce the chance of entanglement, and position it as high above the water as possible to minimize the drag of the current on the rope (see figure 4.14). Normally, the on-shore rope will be managed by a "rope team" of two or more people. The ferrying craft carries only the end of the rope: the paying out process is managed from shore. A kayaker may carry the rope by running it through the stern grab loop and then to the paddle hand, by attaching to the tow system of his kayak, or by clipping it to his rescue harness or life jacket (if it has a quick-release) (see also figure 4.15). A tandem open canoe can carry a third person in the middle to hold the rope. Rafts are often best for ferries like this, because the rope handler can stand if necessary.

Figs. 4.14. The rope ferry. Keep the rope as far out of the water as possible, to minimize drag. The team uses a canoe with a third person to hold the rope high.

Fig. 4.15. This kayaker uses a quick and dirty method of ferrying a rope. He wraps the rope once loosely around his body and holds the end in his teeth. This method is not without risk, nor is it recommended for denture wearers.

Try to keep the rope out of the water during the ferry. On a wide river this can't be done, and you should start the ferry as far upstream as possible to allow for the drag of the current on the rope. The wider and swifter the river, and the larger the diameter of the rope, the more drag there will be, and the maximum amount of drag will occur just when the ferry craft reaches the opposite bank. The ferry craft must therefore drive into the eddy on the opposite shore and attempt to get the rope belayed or lifted clear of the water as soon as possible, otherwise the ferry craft will quickly be pulled back into the current. If possible, station people on the other bank, ready to grab the ferry craft and take the rope when it comes over. A tip for reducing the current's drag on the rope is to use a smaller-diameter line for the initial ferry, then hauling over a heavier rope with it. The 1/4-inch line in some smaller throw bags or even parachute cord will work for this.

Floating Tag Lines. A floating tag line is very useful when a swimmer is caught in a keeper hydraulic like a low-head dam. In a hydraulic like this a person can survive for a surprisingly long time if the water is not too cold and if he does not panic. In many situations like this the victim simply cannot be reached by throw rope or by boat. By timing his breathing and staying relaxed (or as relaxed as one can be in such a situation!), the swimmer may gain enough time for a tag line rescue.

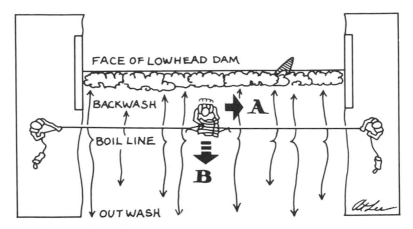

Figs. 4.16. The floating tag line rescue.

Fig. 4.17. A floating tag line. A life jacket provides the buoyant object for the swimmer to grasp.

The first step is to ferry a rope across the river as described earlier. Before beginning the ferry, tie a buoyant object to the middle of the rope for the victim to grasp. A life jacket is suitable. Upon reaching the other side of the river, the ferry team becomes the rope team and, in coordination with the rope team on the other side, moves the buoyant object as required to reach the victim. The efforts should be coordinated by a rescue leader standing in a position visible to all and directing the action with prearranged hand signals.

Once the swimmer has gotten hold of the flotation device, he is normally pulled to one side of the hydraulic and rescued. If this isn't possible, both teams can try moving downstream simultaneously, pulling the swimmer with them, to break the grip of the hydraulic (see figure 4.16).

The tag line rescue is premised on the victim's being conscious and capable of clinging to a floating object. What do you do when the victim is unconscious? The Ohio Department of Natural Resources' Division of Watercraft has developed a flotation ring with unbarbed treble hooks on it to snag an unconscious victim's clothing. The recreational paddler will have to improvise. A method of last resort might be to use a tethered rescuer wearing several life jackets as the buoyant object. This is a desperate measure, posing great danger to the rescuer, and a rescue team should only consider it if they know the victim is alive and no other method will work (see also the "Tethered Boat Rescue" section in chapter 5).

Snag Tags. This variant of the tag line uses a bare or weighted line rather than a buoyant one. It is set up the same way as the floating tag line, but its purpose is to reach an object wholly or partly beneath the surface of the water, such as a pinned boat or an entrapped victim (see figures 4.18 and 4.19). The snag tag does take time to set up, so unless the victim can breathe you should consider it a backup to more quickly arranged methods like the strong-swimmer rescues described later in this chapter.

As we mentioned earlier, an entrapment victim can sometimes push himself to the surface briefly for a breath of air. If so, the rescuers can use a tag line to assist and stabilize him. Speed is essential: do not take time to attach anything to the tag line. Bring the bare line from downstream up to the victim. Once he has the rope he can place his arms over it so that the rope handlers can pull his head and shoulders above the surface of the water. If the current is not too strong they might even be able to pull the victim upstream enough for him to free himself.

Adding a weighted object to the line enables the rescuers to sink the line underwater. By using a weighted snag tag, the rescuers may be able to work the line up under the foot of an unconscious victim to release him. A weighted snag tag takes coordination and a fair amount of physical strength to use effectively, and it requires considerable setup time. It is a technique best used in situations where speed is not critical, such as snagging pinned boats or for body recovery.

What should you use for a weighted object? You might fill two throw bags with small stones and clip them together with a carabiner, or clip an ammo box full of rocks to the middle of the line. Use your imagination.

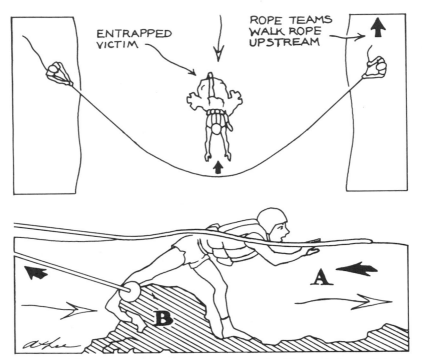

Figs. 4.18. The snag tag rescue. A conscious victim may be able to grab the rope (A). If the victim is unconscious or dead, the rescuers may be able to work the rope under his leg to free his foot (B).

Fig. 4.19. The snag tag in action. Here the rescuers are preparing to sink the line. Controlling a snag tag requires a fair amount of strength.

Controlling the snag tag line is difficult, since the weighted object jumps around in the current like a hooked marlin. To control it, each rope team needs a minimum of two people. For example, say your victim's foot is trapped in the riverbed. Position the weighted object approximately 10 feet upstream of the victim, then slacken the rope to allow the object to pass over the victim's head, sink, and land just downstream of him. The force of the current will push the weighted object downstream before it hits bottom. Being hit by it will be the least of the victim's worries.

When the weighted object hits bottom there will be a small vibration, not unlike that of a fish nibbling bait. This is when the rope needs to be moved back upstream by the rope teams. We say "moved" because the rope teams do not just pull but actually run quickly upstream.

Snag tags have also been used to free pinned boats that are totally submerged. The principle is similar to that of the "rope tricks" and is covered along with pins and extrications in chapter 6.

Strong-Swimmer Rescues

The strong-swimmer type of rescue puts a rescuer in the water to make a contact rescue. The rescuer may be tethered or may hold a rope in order to access the accident site. Strong-swimmer rescues are quick to set up, and by holding the rescue swimmer with a rope, we provide him with some security in the water. But by committing himself to the water, the rescuer unavoidably increases his chances of injury or drowning. If no one's life is in danger, other, and usually slower, shore- or boat-based rescues should be considered first. But sometimes there is no alternative: a life-threatening situation, like that of a paddler entrapped in his boat, demands immediate action, and speed is the major advantage of this method of rescue. Rescuers using this method must sometimes balance the urgent need to rescue a victim against the potential danger to themselves.

For most strong-swimmer rescues, you will need a belayer, a rescue swimmer, and a rescue leader, although it can be done with only a belayer and a rescue swimmer. The leader should position himself so that he is visible to both the swimmer and the belayer and can communicate with them using hand signals. Ideally the rescue swimmer should have a rescue harnesss or life jacket with an attachment point and a quick-release, as described in chapter 2. If that is not available, a *loose* loop of rope passed under the rescuer's armpits will work (see figure 4.20A). The loop should be loose enough to pass over his head and shoulders if he needs to escape quickly and should be tied with a nonslip knot like a bowline. He should also be equipped with a tightly fitted life jacket (or even two), a helmet and wetsuit if they are available, and a knife to cut free of the rope if necessary.

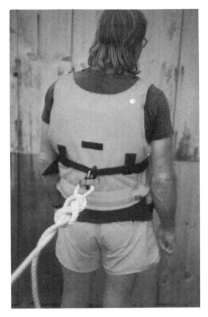

Fig. 4.20. A: Strong swimmer rescues may be executed with a loose loop of rope tied with a bowline and a stopper. Leave plenty of room for the rescuer to slide free of the loop. B: The preferred method, however, is for the swimmer to use a rescue harness (either separate or built into a life jacket) with a quick-release.

The object of the strong-swimmer rescue is usually to get the rescue swimmer into the eddy behind the victim. Frequently the hazard that caused the accident or the pinned boat will itself create an eddy. In some cases the rescue swimmer can be lowered (that is, allowed to float with the current directly to the accident site), while in others he will have to swim aggressively to reach it. He may even wade. In many cases, especially with a rescue life jacket or harness, a swimmer can control his position by angling his body one way or the other in the current. The tethering rope allows the belayers to retrieve the swimmer, but it can cause problems if it snags. A positive release (or knife) is a necessity.

Once the rescue swimmer has reached the accident scene, he should attempt to free the victim, but his first consideration must be to stabilize the situation and keep matters from worsening. The rescue team could set up a tag line to keep a victim's head above water. They could also set up additional lines (pulled over by the rescue swimmer with his own safety line) to keep a pinned boat from moving or to haul it from shore. Once the rescuer and the victim are free, they can be swung in to shore.

Four types of strong-swimmer rescues are described next.

Tethered Swimmer. This rescue is best suited to narrow rivers: the wider the river, the more drag on the belay rope. The rescue swimmer launches himself from a point upstream of the victim, ferries out, and attempts to catch the eddy behind the accident site. This may be a free swim with a slack line, with the rope merely providing a means of retrieval if the swimmer misses the eddy, or the belayer may keep the line taut and attempt to aid the swimmer in maneuvering toward the eddy. The belayer, who may be on either side of the river, is usually located downstream of the launch point but upstream of the victim. The belayer should be able to see the victim and the rescue swimmer at all times. The belay can also be based on midriver boulders or islands if necessary (see figure 4.21).

Midcurrent Lowers. The lowering point is directly upstream of the accident site—on an island, a boulder, a bridge, or a peninsula on a river bend. This method allows more positive control by the belayer and is less risky than the tethered swimmer method (see figure 4.22).

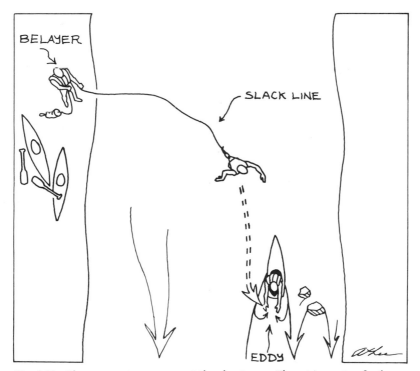

Fig. 4.21. The strong swimmer rescue: tethered swimmer. The swimmer aims for the eddy below the accident site.

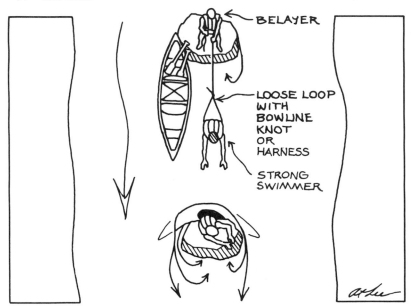

Fig. 4.22. The strong swimmer rescue: midcurrent lower.

The Fixed Line. The rescue team stretches a fixed line across the river at water level. If the water is shallow enough to stand in, the rescuer holds the fixed line at his waist and works his way out on the upstream side of it. When the rescue swimmer reaches a point directly upstream of the victim the belayers slacken the line to lower him to the accident site. As the lowering process continues, the rescue swimmer is held in the apex of the line and his position becomes more and more secure, and since he is not directly attached to the rope he can escape simply by somersaulting and swimming to safety (see figure 4.24).

This method is very quick to set up and requires a minimum of equipment. It is excellent for foot entrapment rescues, which usually occur in shallow water, although it puts the rescuer in potentially the same situation.

A variation of this technique, which works better in deeper and swifter water, is for the rescuer to go out on the rope hand over hand on the downstream side of the rope, and let the current plane his body on the surface, rather than trying to stand. This works best if the rope is set 3–4 feet above the surface of the water and put in tension.

The rope can be ferried across the river by boat or rescue swimmer and should be belayed around a tree or boulder on both shores. If there are not enough people the rope can be tied on one side and belayed on the other, but this is more dangerous to the rescue swimmer. The rescue swimmer can take an auxiliary line out with him if necessary. If he does, someone besides the belayer should hold that line.

Fig. 4.23. The fixed line rescue. The rescuer is held in the apex of the line by the force of the water but is able to swim free by somersaulting over or under the rope.

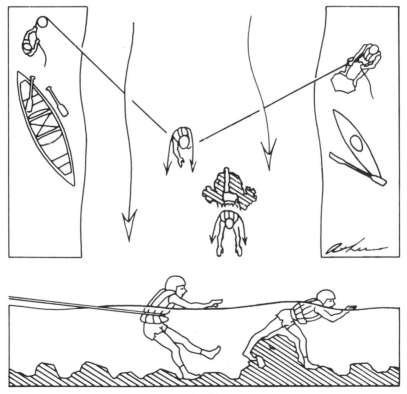

Fig. 4.24. The strong swimmer rescue: fixed line.

The Zip Line or Tension Ferry. The zip line is a single line with moderate tension, stretched diagonally across the river at water level. It is normally used for ferrying rescuers and equipment across a river (in setting up a rescue system, for example) with greater security than swimming. The person crossing clips into the zip line with a small loop of rope attached to a carabiner. He holds the loop (see figure 4.25) and angles his body toward the far shore. The current then pushes him along the line. The zip line can also be used to get a rescuer to an accident site if it can be set to pass near or behind the site and the rescuer is able to stop himself. This technique also works with a raft.

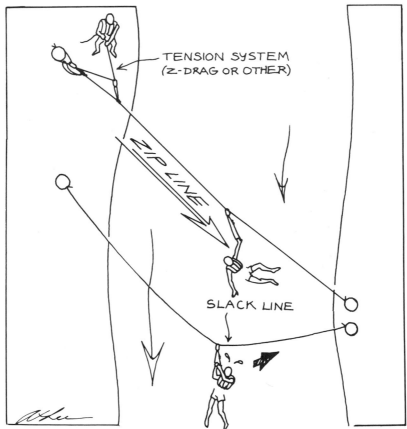

Fig. 4.25. The zip line offers a quick way to move people across a river. Both tension and angle are important: a slack line (below) will strand the person crossing in midcurrent.

Conclusion

No other single rescue tool is as important as the safety rope. It can be used in a wide variety of rescue and evacuation situations. Ropes have their limitations, especially for wider rivers, and should not be used as a crutch or as a substitute for boating rescue skills. Like any other piece of equipment, ropes can be misused, and rescuers should keep the dangers of poor placement and entanglement in mind. Nevertheless, all paddlers, guides, and boatmen should make proficiency with a rope an important part of their river skills.

About the only thing I had learned about canoeing was to head into the part of the rapids that seemed to be moving the fastest, where the most white water was.

JAMES DICKEY, DELIVERANCE

· 5 ·

Boat-based Rescue

One of the fastest and most obvious means of rescue is by boat: a "chase boat" can often be employed more quickly than a shore-based system. The disadvantage is that it is more dangerous to a rescue boater, who must obviously be in the same place as the victim. The harder the water and the less skillful the boater, the lower the chances of success and the greater the chance of ending up with two victims instead of one. A victim clinging to any craft, no matter how cooperative he may be, makes control of the craft more difficult.

Shore- and boat-based rescue techniques are complementary and should be used together. *Where possible,* the primary rescue method should be shore based, since this is safer for the rescuers, with a boat-based rescue as backup. Some factors, such as the width of the river, may obviously force a change in the order of preference or eliminate shore-based rescue entirely, but the idea of using different methods at the same time remains valid.

Rescuing Boaters

Getting the victim out of danger while he is still in his boat makes for a much more controllable situation than if boat, paddle, and paddler must all be rescued separately.

One such method is the Eskimo rescue; it is one of the first techniques a decked-boat paddler learns (see figure 5.1). When upside down, instead of attempting to roll, or perhaps after several attempts to roll, the boater leans forward and slaps the sides of the boat to signal that he needs help. A fellow boater then moves over and presents the bow of his boat to the submerged boater's waiting hands. It is then a simple matter for the upside-down paddler to roll back upright.

Fig. 5.1. The Eskimo rescue. This is a basic technique of decked boat rescue.

The Eskimo rescue has obvious limitations. The upside-down boater may float into rocks or into a more dangerous rapid and draw would-be rescuers in after him. Coming out of the boat is always an honorable alternative, although a much better one is to have a bombproof Eskimo roll. Typically, the Eskimo rescue is limited to places like the deep-water tail waves below a rapid or the eddy just below a hole.

Boats can also be used to rescue other boaters from hydraulics. For small hydraulics the paddler in the rescue boat may stick his bow into the back-wash so that the "stuck" paddler can grab it (see figures 5.2 and 5.3). In larger hydraulics the rescuer may try approaching from upstream with max-imum momentum and drop in sideways onto the stuck boat, knocking it clear of the backwash. This technique presupposes a willingness on the part of the rescue boater to enter the hydraulic the stuck boat has just left.

Neither of these techniques is for the faint of heart.

Rescuing Swimmers

Chase boats should approach swimmers with caution: people who think their lives are in danger often act irrationally. We have seen a panicked swimmer crawl onto a rescuing kayak, tip it over, and then crawl up again onto the upside-down boat, preventing the kayaker from rolling and thus providing the river with an additional victim.

Fig. 5.2. *To rescue another paddler form a small hole, this paddler has given his friend the bow of his boast. By backstroking . . .*

Fig. 5.3. *. . . he gets the paddler but not the boat. Results with this method tend to be unpredictable.*

Decked Boats.   If time permits, the best method is to approach the victim so that you are just out of his reach and try to get his attention. This way you will be able to make some assessment of his mental and physical condition and give him some instructions. Do *not* paddle up alongside the swimmer, because he may grab you or your paddle and tip you over. Appear calm and in control, but be on guard for the unexpected. Offer the swimmer the bow or stern grab loop of your boat. If you're going to tow him any distance, a stern hold makes this easier. Tell the swimmer not to climb upon the boat (there are exceptions to this rule, which we will discuss later) and to help by kicking with his feet (see figure 5.4).

Rescue in a major rapid or in big waves calls for some extra precautions. The violent up-and-down movement of the boat can easily smash a swimmer's face, even if he is hanging on to the grab loop. In a drop-and-pool river it is often better to follow the swimmer and offer assistance at the bottom. Having someone nearby in the rapid can be very heartening, but in big, continuous water this is more difficult. Some boaters use a third grab loop or wooden toggle near the cockpit so that the swimmer can climb onto the rear deck. This avoids the problem of the stern's hitting the victim's face, makes it easier for the victim to breathe in big waves, and somewhat reduces his exposure to cold water. A less satisfactory method, because of the danger of popping the sprayskirt, is for the swimmer to hold on to the cockpit rim. Having an extra person on the back deck makes a boat heavy and unstable, but the victim can assist by kicking with his legs. Before starting, tell the victim to let go of the boat if it tips over, so you can roll.

Normally the rescuers will want to get the victim to shore as quickly as possible, but there are exceptions. For example, if the river is very wide and cold, or if it is flooding out of its banks and through the trees on shore, it may be preferable to get the paddler back in his boat while still on the river. This is relatively easy if the rescuers can get him to a raft, but if not, the rescuers can often form a makeshift raft by holding several boats together, dumping out the swamped craft, and allowing the swimmer to reenter his boat. Paddlers rescued several of their fellows this way during high-water runs of the Potomac in 1985.

Unconscious Victims.   Another problem area, especially for decked boaters, is dealing with an unconscious or semiconscious victim who will quickly drown if left in the water. Rafts and canoes can lift a victim out of the water, but a decked boater cannot without surrendering control of his own craft. There is no ideal solution, but one method is for the rescue boater to come out of his boat and physically assist the victim in the water. This works best in easier water where there are other rescuers, either nearby in boats or on shore with ropes, to help. Another method might be to use the boat's tow

Fig. 5.4. *The basic method of rescuing a swimmer with a kayak is to have the swimmer hang onto the grab loop and kick vigorously with his feet.*

Fig. 5.5. *A swimmer may want to climb up on the back deck of the boat in bigger water. He may grab either the cockpit rim or a loop behind the cockpit.*

system. Some of the tow systems described in chapter 2 can, under certain conditions, tow an unconscious victim with his head more or less out of the water (see figure 5.6). More research is needed in this critical area.

Open Canoes. Since most canoeists cannot roll, they must approach victims with even more caution than would a decked boater. In easier water you can rescue a swimmer by throwing out the stern painter for him to grab. If you have two paddlers, this will increase both your speed and towing power.

The open canoe can be very useful as a basis of the Telfer lower rescue system described later in this chapter. It also performs some of the more mundane tasks of rescue quite well: ferrying ropes, equipment, and people across calm stretches, or acting as a stretcher or shelter in a pinch.

Rafts. Rafts have the potential to produce swimmers in large numbers, and they are slow and hard to manage after they have filled with water and lost one or more crew members. This makes it important to train raft crews in rescue techniques.

The best time to rescue a person who has fallen out of a raft is within the next few seconds. Even in very turbulent water the swimmer is usually near enough to the raft to be reached with a hand, an extended paddle, or an oar. If the raft is in a rapid, only those crew members who are directly involved in the rescue should stop paddling, unless it becomes obvious that more help is needed.

The first thought of a raft crew, assuming the raft itself is not in danger, should be to get the swimmer *back in the raft*: clinging to the side of a raft feels secure, but it can be very dangerous. It is not unusual to see people laughing and talking as they float down the river like this, oblivious to the danger of being caught between the raft and a rock. The best way to pull a

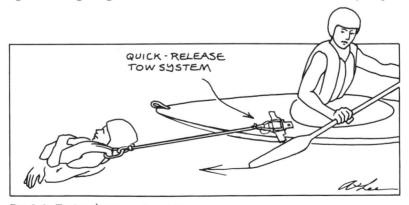

Fig. 5.6. *Towing the unconscious victim.*

Fig. 5.7. Pull a swimmer into a raft by grabbing the shoulder straps of his life jacket and falling back into the raft, not (as the people on the left are doing) by pulling on his arm.

swimmer into a raft is to stand up, brace your knees against the tube, and grab the shoulder straps of the life jacket; then lean back and pull the swimmer in (see figure 5.7). If you grab the swimmer's hands or arms you will only drape his body over the tube. A swimmer can assist by doing a scissors kick and pulling up on a convenient D-ring while being lifted.

If the raft flips on a big river it may be possible for some crew members to climb on top, rescue the other members, and then paddle the upside-down raft to shore.

Boat-Based Rope Rescue. Rafters, and to a lesser extent decked and open boaters, can apply the same principles of rope throwing and positioning outlined in chapter 4 from their boats. This extends the reach of the boat when it is used as a mobile rescue platform and is very useful on wide rivers, or when approaching a victim in a hydraulic who cannot be reached from shore.

Some oar boatmen carry a short (20–30 feet) throw bag for rescue. This is clipped into a convenient D-ring or worn on the boatman's waist; a boatman can make a quick toss and then go back to rowing immediately. The swimmer can then pull himself in or be dragged in by other crew members. A paddle-raft variation is to have a small throw bag secured within easy reach of the raft captain. All such systems need to be attached with a quick-release clip.

A recent innovation is the "Rescue Belt," featuring two 10-foot static lines that can be used for a tow system on a kayak or as a flip line on a raft. The belt also contains 50 feet of rope and can be thrown as a throw bag.

Decked and open boaters can, as mentioned earlier, make limited use of throw bags while in their boats, although the dangers of flipping and entanglement must be kept in mind. Small bags suitable for wearing around the waist are now on the market. If you choose to use one, make sure that you can release it.

Tethered Boat Rescue. In extreme cases, such as a low-head dam rescue, where there is no other alternative, the rescuers may tether both the boat *and the paddler* (in case he comes out of his boat) and send both into the hydraulic (see figure 5.9). The rescue boater must then either physically grab the victim or snag him with a mechanical device such as a paddle hook, whereupon both are pulled from the backwash by the tethering lines. This is similar to the tethered swimmer technique described in the last chapter. A safer variation of this rescue is to send only the tethered boat in.

Equipment Retrieval

Retrieving equipment is often a necessary task on the river. In an emergency, though, people must come before equipment, so you should decide in advance who is to go after what. In most cases it works best for shore-based rescuers to go after people while boaters go after boats, paddles, and equipment: if the shore-based rescue fails the boaters are still in a position to assist. If numbers permit, some boaters can go after equipment while others back up the primary rescue.

Don't risk people, including yourself, for equipment: if you pick up something, be sure you can unload it quickly if need be. Remember to apply the rules of self-preservation: don't run blindly downriver after something without thinking about what lies below.

Paddles. Finding lost paddles is easier than carrying them. Paddlers in rafts and open canoes have few problems, but those in decked boats will find paddles a real nuisance. They can be laid on the cockpit rim of a decked boat, but this only works in easy water. A C-1 paddler who carries a spare paddle on the back deck can put a retrieved paddle underneath the spare. One very simple method of retrieval is to grab the paddle and throw it toward the shore, repeating the process as many times as necessary (see figure 5.10). Kayak paddles are even more of a problem, since they're twice as long. One method is to grasp *both* shafts (that is, yours and the retrieved one) and paddle as if they were one. Sometimes it helps to slide the blades

Fig. 5.8A. The Swiftwater Rescue Belt has two 10-foot static lines that can act as flip lines for rafts or as kayak tow systems.

Fig. 5.8B. The entire belt can also be thrown as a throw bag.

Fig. 5.9. A demonstration of the tethered boat rescue in Austria. Both the boat and the paddler are tethered. Note the paddle hook for snagging the victim.

Fig. 5.10. A simple way to recover paddles on narrow rivers is simply to throw them toward the shore.

out, so that you are only paddling with the blade of one paddle on each side. People with small hands will find this difficult. If your boat has a tow system, you can slide the retrieved paddle under the line on the rear deck and keep one blade "chicken-winged" under an armpit (see figure 5.11).

Boats. The "bulldozer" technique is the most common method of boat recovery, and requires little in the way of special equipment or training (see figure 5.12). The paddler in the recovery boat places his bow on the downstream side of the abandoned boat, sets up as if for a ferry, and then pushes the boat into a convenient eddy. Paddlers recovering decked boats should try to put their bow inside the cockpit of the swamped boat, making sure they will be able to withdraw if the need arises. Open canoes and rafts sometimes have a problem keeping contact with a partly submerged boat.

A decked boat can often be flipped back upright before it fills completely with water, which makes it much easier to handle: if there is not much water in it a good shove can send it into a nearby eddy. Open canoes can also be recovered this way, and unless the boat is completely swamped it is definitely advantageous to try to turn it upright.

A safer and better way to recover a boat is to tow it in with a towing system or painter (see chapter 2), because the recovering boat can stay upstream and avoid being caught between the swamped boat and a rock

Fig. 5.11. A more elegant method of recovery is to use the boat's tow system. The blade can be "chicken-winged" under the paddler's arm to hold it, and the paddle can be released quickly in an emergency.

Fig. 5.12. Most paddlers use the "bulldozer" method to recover boats. It's convenient but has its limitations. A half-submerged boat, like this one, can be difficult to push. Tow systems work better.

(see figures 5.13 and 5.14). Tow systems are not yet widely used in the United States by recreational paddlers. You do see them on the decks of instructors' boats and on expedition boats—these paddlers cannot afford to lose a boat on some remote river. However, tow systems have many applications other than boat rescue; they are easier to hang onto than grab loops if you are swimming; they can be used to haul a boat up an embankment or tie it off in the water; and they make an ideal system for ferrying a line across the river for many of the rescue methods described in this book. As the word spreads, tow systems will undoubtedly become more popular.

The Telfer Lower

The Telfer lower is a mixed system of rescue: it uses a boat or boats but is controlled partially from shore. Use the Telfer lower to reach a fixed accident site when more conventional means of rescue (like rope throws, ferries, and tag lines) are not feasible or have failed. Even in very swift water it provides a surprisingly stable platform from which to rescue a trapped victim or a pinned boat. A working platform made with a raft or a combination of boats is attached to an anchor line stretched across the river and is floated downstream the accident site or into an eddy below it. The Telfer may also be set up with the anchor line just upstream of the accident site, and the rescue craft pulled up to it, or even as a "reverse Telfer," which lowers the

Fig. 5.13. Using the cam cleat tow system: the painter on the tow boat is run through the other boat's grab loop and then secured with the cam cleat . . .

Fig. 5.14. . . . and then the boat is towed away. All tow systems should have a quick-release.

rescue craft *upstream* into the backwash of a hydraulic. The disadvantages of this method are that it takes time to set up and taxes the technical skills and leadership of the rescuers. It also requires a substantial amount of equipment, particularly rope.

To set up a Telfer, first establish an anchor line across the river. This is usually 20–50 feet upstream of the accident site. Allow enough room (and rope) for the rescue craft to float down past the obstacle and come up in the eddy below. You can throw the anchor rope across a narrow river or ferry it across a wide one. The anchor line should be tight and 8–10 feet above the surface of the water. Trees usually make the best anchor points, but you can use boulders, car bumpers, or other fixed objects instead. The anchor line should be angled downstream, so that the current will carry the rescue craft toward the accident site.

The rescue craft can be constructed in a variety of ways. A raft, works well in heavy water, as long as it is fully inflated and rigged with stout D-rings. A cataraft (see chapter 10) may well be the ideal craft for the Telfer, since it provides a stable, unswampable platform that offers little resistance to the current.

Boat Systems. Two open canoes can be lashed together catamaran-style about a foot apart, using saplings or paddles to keep them together (see figures 5.15 and 5.16). They will resist the current less than a raft but are more likely to swamp. A canoe and a kayak can be used, as can three kayaks. A single boat will also work, but it will not be as stable as a raft or two boats.

The heart of the Telfer lower is the carabiner chain or pulley system, which provides a flexible joint that will slide easily on the anchor line. The upper pulley (or carabiner) slides on the anchor line, while the lower pulley (or carabiner) serves to lower the rescue craft to the accident site. A rope loop (such as a prusik loop), or locking carabiner, links the two and provides a tie-in point for tag lines. The tag lines control the left-to-right position of the rescue craft in the current.

There are three methods for lowering the rescue craft to the victim:

1. *Belayer on shore.* The rope is attached to the boat and run through the lower carabiner to the shore party, who belay according to instructions from the boat (see figure 5.17). This method allows the rescuers in the craft to concentrate their efforts on the victim or boat but requires a substantial amount of rope—you cannot easily use two ropes joined together, since a knot will not pass through most carabiners. There may be communication problems

Fig. 5.15. The Telfer lower ready to go. The rescue craft is made with two canoes lashed together. Note that the anchor line is angled downstream so that the current pushes the boat toward the rescue site.

Fig. 5.16. This rescue craft is lashed together with paddles. Saplings would work better. This craft is set up for a direct lower as shown in figure 5.20. Note the V-harness on the bow to keep the craft straight.

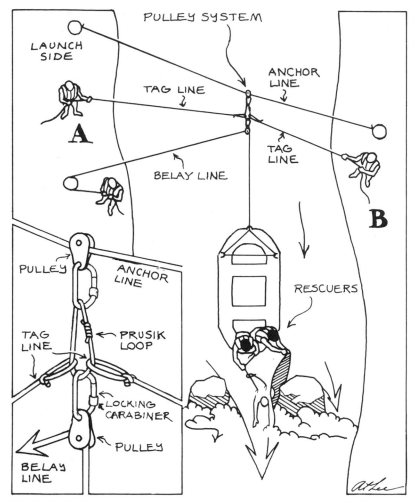

Fig. 5.17. The Telfer lower: belayer on shore. Tag line A may be eliminated if the rescuers are short-handed. The pulley system shown in the inset is superior to the carabiner chain shown in figure 5.20.

between the shore party and the rescue craft, and pulling on or releasing the lowering line will make the rescue craft move side to side as well as up and down. This method requires practice and coordination.

2. *Belayer in the rescue craft.* The lowering rope is attached to the rescue craft, runs through the lower pulley, and then runs back to the rescue craft (see figure 5.18 and 5.19). This method gives the rescuers precise control and eliminates the communication problems of the first method. Pulling through the lower pulley

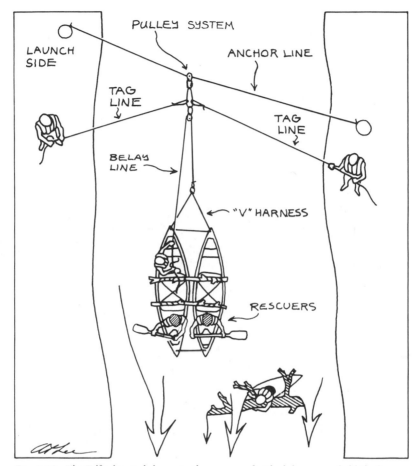

PULLEY SYSTEM

LAUNCH SIDE

ANCHOR LINE

TAG LINE

TAG LINE

BELAY LINE

"V" HARNESS

RESCUERS

Fig. 5.18. The Telfer lower: belayer in the rescue craft. The belayer may hold the line or use the thwart as a belay point.

against a V-harness rigged to the front of the craft gives excellent directional stability. It requires less rope than the first method but more than the third. This is probably the easiest system for the rescuers to operate.

3. *Belayer in the rescue craft.* The rope is tied to the lower carabiner and the rescue craft is belayed directly by the rescuer (see figures 5.20 and 5.21). A directional carabiner must be rigged at the front of the boat to keep it straight in the current. Of the three methods, this requires the least rope but may have directional stability problems in the current. Belay by wrapping the rope around a D-ring, around a thwart, or through a locking carabiner using a Münter hitch.

The choice of method employed will depend on the number of people, the number and type of boats, the amount of rope available, as well as the distance the rescue craft must be lowered.

Even with the attached tag lines, the crew of the rescue craft must have paddles to control the angle of the craft and to paddle it out if the system fails. All rescuers should have life jackets and knives. Use prearranged hand signals to coordinate the movements of the boat. There should be a team leader in the boat, but the rescue leader should remain on shore if possible to oversee the entire operation. Someone should stand upstream of the rescue site to warn off other boaters, and others should be rope throwers downstream. Put the best paddlers in the boat.

Fig. 5.19. The whitewater sleigh ride! This version of the Telfer uses the belayer in the rescue craft. The rope is run from the carabiner on the V-harness in the bow to the lowering carabiner and then back to the belayer in the boat.

The most critical part of the rescue is the launch, since it is here that the rescue craft is most likely to run into trouble. Make sure the bow of the boat remains pointed directly upstream, because if the boat swings broadside to the current it may swamp. If the boat does get swamped, the belayer and the tag line team should try to pendulum the boat ashore. If this is not possible, the rescue craft must be released, and there must be no knots or bags on the line to impede the release if this is necessary. The rescue crew should not hesitate to cut the rope.

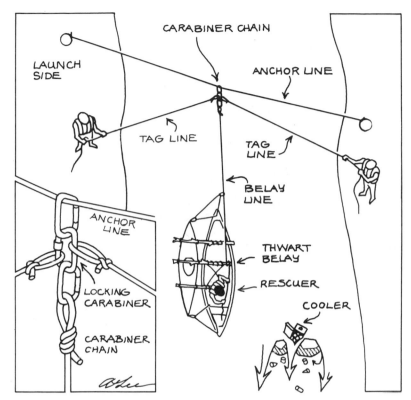

Fig. 5.20. The Telfer lower: the rescue craft is lowered or raised with a single line attached to the carabiner chain.

Since it is dangerous for the rescuers to be on the upstream side of the accident site, they should attempt to let the rescue craft float past the obstacle and raise it in the eddy behind.

Raft Systems. Rafts use a somewhat different rigging system. It is important that the raft be loaded in the stern so that the bow will plane over the surface of the water. A front-loaded raft will ship water and is hard to control. Rafts also offer considerably more resistance to the current than do canoes, so that it is usually best to belay them from the stern of the raft using a Münter hitch (see figure 5.22). In a short-handed rescue, a slip knot above the Münter hitch will lock it off while the rescuer deals with the accident. Rafts can also be moved back upstream this way. One person hauls on the upstream side of the hitch while another takes up the slack. It is slow and difficult work.

Fig. 5.21. The direct lower with the belayer in the rescue craft. The belayer can either hold the rope directly, as here, or use a friction belay.

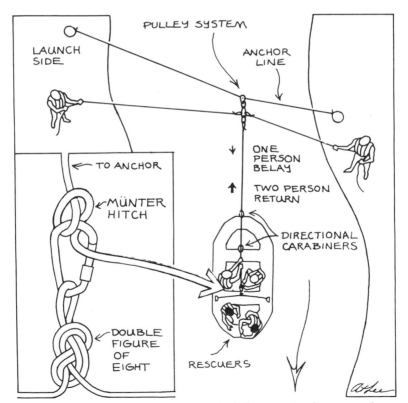

Fig. 5.22. The Telfer lower, using a Münter hitch for positioning the rescue craft upstream or downstream.

Conclusion

Under the right conditions, boat-based rescue is very effective; in some situations (on very wide rivers, for example) it will be the primary rescue system. Boat-based rescue can also be effectively integrated with shore-based rope systems, and rescuers should use the two systems to back each other up. A tow system is a useful addition to any boat.

The Telfer lower uses elements of both systems and can be used effecively both as a rescue platform and as a means of ferrying patients across rivers during evacuations.

Wherein I spake of most disastrous chances, Of moving accidents by flood and field, Of hair-breadth 'scapes i' the imminent deadly breach.
WILLIAM SHAKESPEARE, *OTHELLO*

· 6 ·
Entrapments and Extrications

A group of expert paddlers went out on North Carolina's Watauga River in the spring. The Watauga is steep, with almost continuous rapids, many big drops, and a 15-foot waterfall. "You had to catch every eddy in order to boat scout the next rapid," one member of the group recalls, "and we didn't know exactly where the waterfall was." As it turned out, the eddy that one of the paddlers missed was the one just above the waterfall. He went down backward over the wrong chute and pinned half-way down the falls on a small boulder.

Fortunately, he was with an alert, experienced group of paddlers. They immediately sized up the situation, got out of their boats, and went after him. The entrapped paddler was able to breathe, but the water was very cold. Though he was dressed for the season, hypothermia was an immediate danger. His legs were entrapped under the thwart seat in his low-volume C-1. The rescuers were able to wade out to the boulder, at some danger to themselves, and hold the victim's head out of the water. "Finally," said one of the rescuers, "we were able to pull him up enough to let him slide his legs out from under the thwart and get free. But it was touchy, and he wouldn't have lasted long in that cold water."

Here we have the classic elements of both a boat pin and an entrapment: a good paddler in hard water making only a small mistake. In this case there was a happy ending, but it was only because of the quick and correct actions of the rescuers.

Entrapments and Boat Pins

People are entrapped; boats are pinned. "Entrapped" means being held in a life-threatening position by the force of the water or by a collapsed boat; a boat is "pinned" when it is held in place against a solid object by the force of the current. Since an entrapment is often a direct result of a pin, we will discuss them together here. (Foot entrapment is discussed along with rescue methods in chapter 4.)

Not all paddlers are pinned in their boats; recently there have been cases in which paddlers who bailed out of their pinned or broached boats had their bodies entrapped on the same obstacle that held the boat.

Boat pins fall into two main categories: broaches and vertical pins.

Broaches. A boat broaches when it wraps sideways around an obstacle, usually a bridge piling, a boulder, or a tree (see figure 6.1). There is usually a cushion of water on the upstream side of an obstacle, and the river-wise paddler can normally ride over this "pillow" and avoid a direct collision. Some obstacles, however, like bridge pilings and undercut rocks, have little or no upstream cushion and are much more dangerous to approach.

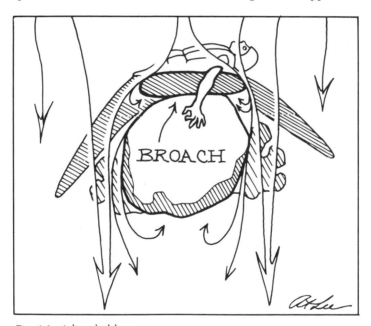

Fig. 6.1. A broached boat.

The fatal moment of the broach occurs when the boat collapses and entraps the paddler. This most often happens to kayakers—the front deck collapses on their legs—but rafts and canoes can entrap people as well.

Vertical Pins. A boat is vertically pinned when the bow slams into the riverbed and stays (see figure 6.2). It is most common on steep, ledgy, shallow rivers. Paddling drops of more than 4 or 5 feet invites a vertical pin, but paddling technique and boat design also play a part. A paddler may reduce the risk of pinning by "ski-jumping" the boat so that it "pancakes" at the bottom of the drop—that is to say, he goes off the drop with a lot of forward speed and leans back radically as the boat starts to drop, causing it to land flat on the bottom of the hull rather than burying the bow. Though this is a useful technique, it can cause severe back injuries.

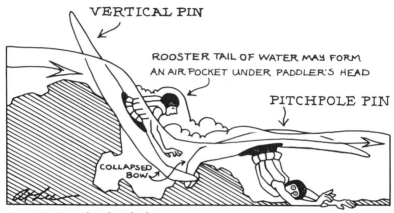

Fig. 6.2. Vertical and pitchpole pins.

On the whole, a low-volume needle-nosed design is more prone to pinning vertically than is a higher-volume blunt-bowed one. In Europe a whole class of extreme descent boats (typified by the "Topolino") has emerged for steep alpine runs. These boats are very short (some as short as 6 feet) and have very large cockpits and blunt, rounded, bows. Similar boats are available in the United States now, and they are certainly the boat of choice for steep creeks. Another alternative is to use some of the older large-volume cruising designs.

When the bow is wedged into rocks or under a submerged tree, the force of the water will quickly produce catastrophic results: the boat may "pitchpole" and collapse at the fulcrum created by the obstacle, but a more common result is for the water to force the stern of the boat to the bottom too, collapsing it along with the buried bow. Even if the boat does not actually fold, the paddler may be held inside the boat by the sheer force of the current against his back. If the water is not too deep he may be able to form an air pocket in front of his body by pushing up on the front deck. This is very tiring, especially in cold water, and rescue efforts must begin immediately.

C-1s (decked canoes) are often cited as being less likely to entrap a paddler than a kayak. Since the paddler's legs are tucked under him, so the argument goes, he has less exposure that does a kayaker, whose legs are fully extended. With today's low-volume canoe designs, however, this is no longer entirely true. In a small boat, particularly one with a thwart rather than a pedestal seat, a canoeist's feet can be entrapped by the collapse of the *rear* deck. Open canoes are less vulnerable to entrapments, but they are certainly not immune. One open-boat paddler spent over two hours under Sweet's Falls on the Gauley River after pinning in the drop; the boat collapsed, pinning one of his legs between the crushed hull and a thwart. Another canoeist nearly drowned on the Ocoee river after broaching his canoe on a bridge piling. He became entangled in his thigh straps and had to be cut out by a rescue party (see chapter 7).

Entrapment Rescues

An entrapment rescue generally proceeds in four stages: assessment, stabilization, extrication, and evacuation. For a more in-depth discussion of rescue organization and methods, see chapter 8.

Assessment. This is the critical first step: the most important question is whether it is a "head-up" or "head-down" entrapment: if the victim can breathe you can afford a few more minutes to decide on and use the best and safest method of rescue; if the victim's head is under water you must react immediately.

Stabilization. The rescuers must first stabilize both the condition of the victim and the position of the boat. Don't charge blindly into trying to remove the victim before you have made sure both are stable. Be careful about popping the boat's sprayskirt until you are sure the situation is stabilized, since this will fill the boat with water, and the result may be unpredictable. Ensure first that the victim can continue to breathe; then see that the boat does not shift and make the situation worse.

If the entrapment site is accessible, the quickest and most obvious way to stabilize the situation is with a contact or "hands-on" method like the one described at the beginning of this chapter. Consider whether the rescuers can stand on or at least near the obstacle that created the entrapment, or on the pinned boat itself. If they cannot stand in the current, can they wade out on a fixed line or be pendulumed or lowered down to the accident site with a strong-swimmer rescue (as discussed in chapter 4) and hold the victim's head up? Can a rope from shore or a tag line be rigged to keep the victim's head above water? And should auxiliary lines be tied to the pinned boat to keep it from shifting?

If the rescuers cannot get close to the victim, another possibility is to use a floating tag line (see chapter 4). Bring the tag line up from the downstream

Fig. 6.3. A rescuer rigs a line to keep the victim's head above water.

side, so that the victim can drape his arms over it, then pull it upstream to help keep his head up (see figure 6.4). Even if the victim cannot hear or see under a rooster tail of water, the tag line will provide the psychological boost to let him know someone is out there trying to help.

Extrication. The extrication process should not start until the victim has been stabilized in a relatively safe position. If he cannot be stabilized, however, as with a head-down pin, you must begin extrication efforts immediately.

With a contact rescue (like that described at the beginning of this chapter) one or more rescuers may physically assist the victim in getting out. Consider also whether the boat can be cut to facilitate releasing the victim. Modern boat materials make this difficult without the proper tool (see chapter 2), but with a raft this may be the logical solution. Most extrications, however, will involve attaching lines to the pinned craft and then using shore-based power to pull the boat free. (Methods of extricating pinned boats are discussed in more detail in the "Boat Recovery" section in this chapter, and the various rope tricks discussed later can also be used to stabilize or extricate a victim.)

Foot entrapment situations are similarly handled. The normal way to extricate a victim whose foot is entrapped is to use a floating tag line, a snag tag, or a strong-swimmer rescue (see chapter 4).

Evacuation. The final stage of an entrapment rescue is the evacuation of the victim—who may now be a patient—from the accident site to shore. Monitor his condition continuously from the time the rescuers reach the scene and continue to do so throughout the evacuation. Use CPR and first aid as necessary.

You should give some thought to the evacuation of the patient while you are involved in extricating him. If the patient is coherent and uninjured, you might simply swing him in with a rope; if he is injured, but has been rescued from immediate danger, you should use other, slower methods for evacuation. You might pick him up with a raft or another boat or by means of a Telfer lower. If the situation requires it, he might even be evacuated by helicopter directly from the entrapment site (see chapter 9).

Entrapment Rescue Techniques

Contact Rescue. The rescue described at the beginning of this chapter is a contact rescue. It is a hands-on approach with no rope between rescuer and victim. This is almost always the fastest—and the most dangerous—way to reach an entrapment victim if the rescuers are able to wade, swim, or lower themselves to the accident site. If the victim's head is under water, time is

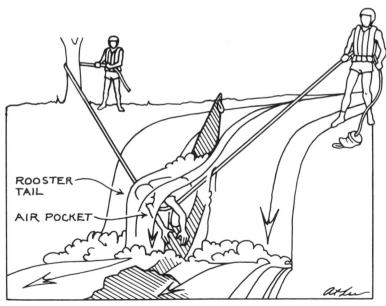

ROOSTER TAIL

AIR POCKET

Fig. 6.4. A stabilization tag line can be set up to keep the pinned paddler's head up while other rescue methods are used to extricate him.

critical, and this is usually the first method to consider. If the victim can breathe, consider a safer method first. Contact rescues are best done by experienced paddlers or guides who are used to working in the water. Tethering the rescuers (as with a rescue harness) can add an extra measure of safety.

Broach Rescue. The rescuers must get the entrapped paddler's legs out. This job will be much easier if the boat has a large cockpit and stout walls. Remember that popping the sprayskirt may alter the boat's balance and weight dramatically. In less serious situations the rescuers may be able to grab the victim with a bear hug from behind and pull him free. Rocking the boat up and down, first on one end and then the other, may cause it to wash off the obstacle.

If time permits, the rescuers may attach haul lines to the boat and try to pull it free of the obstacle as described later in this chapter. If the boat is equipped with a broach loop (see figure 2.20), a shore-based haul system might lift the deck enough for the victim to slide his legs out. If these methods do not work, the rescuers may choose to cut or saw the boat. Although the rescuer's first thought will usually be to cut the deck to release the victim's legs, a slip of the knife can result in severe injury to the rescuer or the trapped paddler. A better solution sometimes is to cut the boat across the rear of the cockpit so that the victim can be pulled backward out of the boat. Cutting off all or part of the stern may cause the boat to pivot off the obstacle and release the paddler.

Vertical Pin Rescue. In many vertical pins the paddler is not actually entrapped, as in a broach, but rather is held in the boat by a combination of gravity and water pushing against his back. If you want to see how difficult escape in this situation is, get in a kayak, stand it upright on the bow, and try to pull yourself out. A C-1 is much easier to get out of in a vertical pin, since the paddler can simply dive forward.

If the victim can breathe, the rescuers should first stabilize a vertically pinned boat by attaching lines to it so that it cannot shift. A pin is often much more "touchy" than a broach, which means that the rescuers should take the time to set up the best pull and consider the consequences carefully. For the same reason, they should avoid popping the sprayskirt if possible. Use a tag line (figure 6.4) to assist the paddler in keeping his head up. Often the biggest problem with a vertically pinned decked boat is attaching haul lines to it, since it presents a smooth surface with few attachment points (see the section below). It helps if the boat is equipped with a broach loop and sturdy grab loops. Unfortunately, many commercially produced boats have grab loops that are inadequate for hauling the boat out with. At some point the rescuers must either pull the paddler up enough to get him out of the boat, either physically or with a tag line, or they must pull the boat out of the pin—usually the same way it went in. If they can reach the bow (unlikely in a severe pin) they might try to cut away the pinned part of the boat to get it free.

Getting out of boat doesn't necessarily improve the paddler's chances—he may then swim into a body entrapment. For this reason, if possible, the rescuers should try to have a positive hold on the victim, either physically or with a rope, during the extrication. Give some thought to where the extricated victim might end up.

Rigging for Vertical Pins. In the vertical pin section we posed the question of how we might *attach* a rope to an inaccessible boat or victim—one that is pinned where there are no convenient eddies or boulders from which to base a contact rescue. Once the line is attached, the rescuers can use any shore-based haul system, from a simple direct pull to a Z-drag, to pull the boat off.

First they must get to the pinned craft, for which they might use an overhead or vertical rescue, such as a Tyrolean or bridge lower; a Telfer lower; or even a strong-swimmer. The first two methods, which are discussed elsewhere, require a fair amount of time, equipment, and knowledge to set up, and have definite setup limitations. A faster alternative is to use technical rescue equipment such as paddler-carried throw bags and paddle hooks or "rope tricks" (discussed in the next section). The rescuers might also use the rigging systems described later in this chapter, if time permits.

Some European paddlers carry a small throw bad attached to the life jacket or rescue harness to throw out to rescuers if the boat is pinned. This is certainly the fastest method of getting a line on the paddler, and it eliminates many of the problems (like cinching down on the victim's body) associated with the rope tricks. Clipping this line to a broach loop might work even better. This is the method used by the open canoeist pinned at Sweet's Falls on the Gauley River (mentioned earlier in the chapter): he was able to tie his throw bag onto a thwart and let it float out to his companions.

A quick and simple method for attaching a haul line to a decked boat is to use a carabiner ("rescue" versions, which have a larger opening, are especially good for this) hooked over the cockpit rim, then running the line around the boat. Rescuers may also puncture the boat at the cockpit rim, then thread the haul line through the hole. Another method is to use a paddle hook (see chapter 2), which can give the rescuers enough extra reach on a narrow river to get the hook into the grab loop, cockpit rim, or paddler's safety harness. One Austrian manufacturer even makes a harness specifically designed to be "hooked" (see figure 6.5).

Fig. 6.5. Unpinning a boat using a paddle hook. Here two kayak paddles are joined together with special clamps in order to extend the reach of the rescuers. A haul line is attached directly to the paddle hook, which is then hooked on to the pinned boat's grab loop. Note the rescue harness worn over the rescuer's life jacket. It is designed to have a paddle hook slid in between the two pieces of webbing which go over the paddler's shoulders.

Rope Tricks. *Rope trick* is a general term that describes methods of using the current to carry a rope around a boat or victim. Take the example of a kayaker caught in a vertical pin: the boat and the body of the paddler disrupt the current and are frequently out of the water entirely. An appropriate rope trick would be to throw or ferry a rope to the upstream side of the boat and let it float around it. A boat or swimmer could then be used to retrieve the downstream end of the rope and return it to the same shore, thus making a loop of rope around the boat or victim.

In many pins and entrapments the only way to pull a boat and victim out is the way they went in. Similarly, in really inaccessible situations the only way to get a rope to them is often to let the same current that put them there carry the rope. (This was the method finally used to get a rope around Rick Bernard's pinned kayak in the incident described in the prologue, after all other methods had failed.)

Once the loop has been formed, there are several options for cinching down the rope, but the very flexibility of the rope-trick concept prevents our

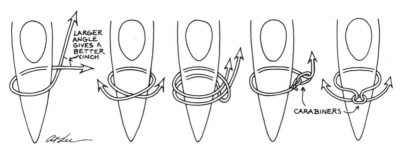

Fig. 6.6. Rope tricks: there are several ways to cinch the rope down on the boat.

showing every variation (see figure 6.6). For example, if a boat were vertically pinned really close to shore, a paddler with a cowboy background
might attempt to throw a lasso over the boat!

If possible, haul on the boat rather than on the victim, since even if the
line is padded it is likely to injure the latter. If the situation is grave enough,
there may be no other choice, though, but to use a cinching rope loop on
the victim's trunk area. In such cases, there is a rope trick (the NOC knot
trick) that can be used to reduce the likelihood of injury (see figure 6.7). Tie
a knot approximately 3–4 feet from what will be the victim's end of the
rope. You can use any type of loop knot—for example, a butterfly or double
figure-of-eight knot. Then form a loop, using a carabiner tied to the end of
the haul line. As the carabiner slides down the haul line the knot will stop it
and create a fixed-diameter loop for the victim. The rescuers should pad the
line and attempt to place the loop around the victim's waist. The knot will
prevent the line from cinching down and restricting breathing. Injury is still
likely using this method, however, and you should not use it unless it is the
only way to rescue the victim.

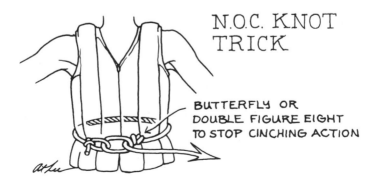

N.O.C. KNOT
TRICK

BUTTERFLY OR
DOUBLE FIGURE EIGHT
TO STOP CINCHING ACTION

Fig. 6.7. The NOC knot trick.

If floating lines can't be used, because the force of the current or the depth of the submerged boat is too great, the rescuers can try a weighted line. You can use an ammo box or throw bag weighted with rocks, just as you did with the snag tag. If the weighted object must slide, clip it into the line with a carabiner.

Recovering Pinned Boats

Extricating a pinned boat can be an interesting project—so long as there is no victim involved and the safety of the group does not depend on success. Usually the damage has been done and there is little need for haste. Opinions can be exchanged, options weighed, and the time taken to make sure everyone understands the retrieval plan. Since time is not critical, use the safest means of extrication, bearing in mind not only your own group but also other paddlers on the river. Try the simplest methods first; go on to more complex systems if the simpler ones fail. Often it is a combination of techniques that works best.

The quickest and simplest method is just to grab the boat and start pulling (the "armstrong" method). This works best if you can safely stand on the river bottom or on the obstacle causing the pin (see figure 6.8). A strong back, or several, helps. Often, lifting one end of the boat while jumping up and down on the other will work. Most people's legs are stronger than their arms, and it may be more effective to sit on the obstacle and push with your legs. If you do this, though, don't let yourself slip down between the boat and the obstacle.

Sometimes a simple lever, such as an oar or a tree limb, can be used to pry the boat off the obstacle. A rope can be tied to the high end and run to shore for additional people to pull on. Tie a backup rope to the boat to swing it in to shore when it comes loose.

Rigging

As we have already mentioned, often the hardest part of a boat recovery is getting the rope attached to the boat. If the current was strong enough to pin the boat, it is probably too strong to stand in safely. Working around pinned boats in swift water is risky and demands caution: the boat may shift at any time but is especially likely to do so under tension from the haul line.

A pinned boat will usually be near the surface, and you can often stand on the boat itself or on the obstacle that caused the pin. If you cannot, you will have to try another method of reaching the pinned craft, such as a Telfer lower or any of the other methods, such as paddle hooks, mentioned in the earlier sections. A completely submerged boat, on the other hand, presents a real problem. Sometimes you can use branches or paddles to push the

Fig. 6.8. The "armstrong" method will work in a lot of cases. Just grab the boat and start pulling. Give some thought to what will happen after the boat comes free.

rope under the boat and then retrieve the loose end on the downstream side of the boat. You can also drop lines weighted with throw bags or ammo boxes stuffed with rocks above the boat and pull them out below with the T-grip of a paddle.

Thwarts on canoes and grab loops on decked boats are obvious points of attachment. On rafts a thwart is sometimes a stronger attachment point than a D-ring. Nevertheless, it is sometimes better, if the boat is severely pinned, to encircle the boat with the line rather than attach the line to a single point. If the thwarts, grab loops, or D-rings are missing or inaccessible, this is your only choice. One quick method of encircling the boat or attaching a line to a raft thwart is simply to tie a carabiner to the end of the line, pull it around the boat, and clip it into the line (see figure 6.11). Another, more destructive method is to puncture the floor of the raft and tie the haul line around the tube (see figure 6.32). This is easy with a self-bailing raft. You can also use a cradle rig; made up of two loops of rope, each of which is smaller in diameter than the widest point of the boat. Slip these over both ends of the boat and connect them with another piece of rope. Attach the haul line to the connecting piece (figure 6.12).

Open canoes and rafts typically pin with the open side upstream and the bottom against the obstacle. If possible, roll the boat over as you pull it off the obstacle, so as to dump the water and reduce the "sea anchor" effect. One way to do this is to attach the rope at the low end of a thwart, pass the rope between the hull and the rock, and pull so that the water spills out.

Fig. 6.9. Sometimes you'll be lucky enough to have a big flat rock to work on; sometimes you can even tie into the canoe's thwarts.

Fig. 6.10. Other times there may not be any thwarts, and you'll have to make a cradle rig.

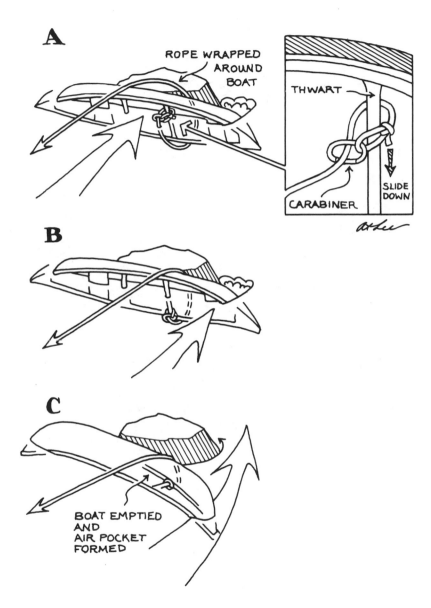

Fig. 6.11. *A carabiner clipped into the end of a line to form a loop is a quick way to attach a line to a thwart.*

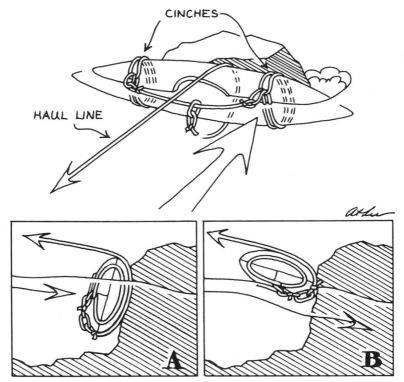

Fig. 6.12. *Use a cradle rig on boats without thwarts.*

With rafts, attach the haul line to the D-ring closest to the river bottom but on the far side of the boat (figure 6.13). As you pull, the rope will apply a rotating force (torque) on the raft and cause it to rotate on its axis as it dumps the water out. The Steve Thomas rope trick does the same thing with a canoe (see figure 6.14).

If you find you cannot dump the water out of a raft, consider deflating one or more of the compartments. Air valves can be bled underwater without getting water in the tubes, as long as the air pressure is greater than the water pressure. If you have good stream of bubbles, the air pressure is adequate. As a last resort, cut through the floor of the raft to reduce the force of the current. This may free the raft, but will mean repair time later. Most pinned rafts can be freed without cutting the floor.

The Force of the Current

When rigging for boat recovery, many people forget to consider the force and direction of the current. Time and again we have seen elaborate sys-

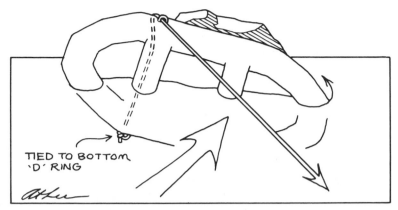

Fig. 6.13. *Pinned boats should also be rigged to flip and dump the water as they're rolled out. (See also figures 6.11 and 6.12.)*

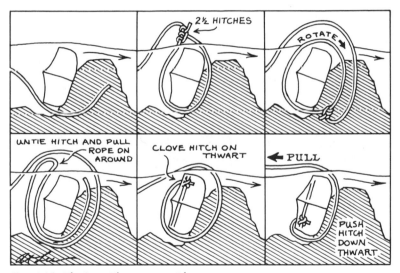

Fig. 6.14. *The Steve Thomas rope trick.*

tems based on convenient anchor points or work areas rather than angle of pull. To some extent, of course, the direction of any pull is dictated by where you can anchor it, but the idea is to make the river work for you. Keep trying: sometimes only a small change in the angle of pull (such as with a vector pull) will make the difference.

Remember a few simple guidelines. First, there is a lot of force out there, and you want it working for and not against you. Avoid pulling directly against the current. Second, get the pinned craft away from the water, either by lifting it or by dumping the water. Third, the water tends to create a force equilibrium on the pinned craft by pushing more or less equally on the parts of it that are underwater. If you can upset this equilibrium, sometimes even by a tiny amount, the craft will often wash off without further pulling. Fourth, do not blindly trust mechanical devices, no matter how powerful they are. A common mistake is to assume that the problem is simply not enough pull. Boats are just not designed to be tugged on with several thousand pounds of force, and a powered winch or a well-set-up haul system can literally pull a boat to pieces (see figure 6.15).

If the situation permits, several ropes pulling from different directions are often more effective than a single rope. Use multiple rigging to avoid pulling directly against the current. One solution is to use the main haul line to counteract the force of the current on the boat and then *slide* the boat sideways until it clears the obstacle. Another line might be used to flip the boat and to dump the water out of it, as previously described. Such a system is detailed in figure 6.16.

When possible, combine hauling systems. The vector pull, for example, can be a useful addition to any of the haul systems described below. It will give some mechanical advantage as well as changing the angle of pull (see figure 6.17).

If you are working with stretchy polypropylene ropes, have the rescuers stand clear of hauling systems: if a D-ring pops loose it can (and has) injured people. The rescuers hauling on the rope should wear life jackets, and they may choose to use a snubbing system (see figure 6.18).

To change the direction of pull, use a directional pulley. This allows the hauling team to pull in the most convenient direction, even if the accident site would not otherwise allow it (see figure 6.19 and 6.20A). One imaginative group of rescuers put the pulley on a tree limb *above* the pinned canoe, enabling them to use their body weight to pull directly down on the haul line.

Haul Systems

Most systems of recovery other than the "armstrong" method use a rope or line attached to the boat. These are collectively called haul systems. The systems described here are meant to get the boat off the obstacle. Remember to consider what will happen once the boat comes free, since water-filled boats, particularly rafts, are very heavy. It's very easy to pull a boat off one obstacle only to have it get into a worse pin on another farther downstream. Backup belay lines to control the craft when it comes free are often needed *in addition to* the haul lines.

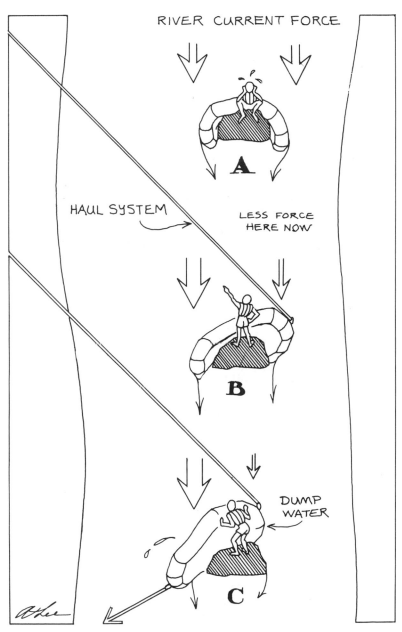

Fig. 6.15. *The force of the water: In (A), the current pushes more or less equally on both ends of the pinned boat, wrapping it against the rock. Pulling at approximately a 45-degree angle to the current in (B) reduces the effective force against one side of the boat, causing the current to push the boat around the other side of the rock (C). Pulling one end up out of the water will do the same thing (see figures 6.31 and 6.32).*

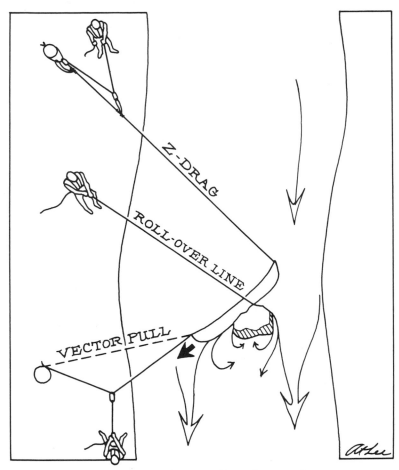

Fig. 6.16. Several haul lines are often more effective than a single one. Here a Z-drag is used to pull the boat away from the rock, while another line is used to roll the boat and dump the water. A third line slides the boat along the face of the rock and into an eddy.

"Ten Boy Scouts" Method.   This is a simple rope pull with no mechanical advantage: attach the rope to the boat, find the best angle to pull from, and pull. If it doesn't move, just add more Boy Scouts. This is the most common method of extrication and is easily integrated with other systems. the force of a direct pull can be increased up to the breaking strength of the rope by using a mechanical device like a "come-along" or winch. Most recreational paddlers don't carry these, but they may be available if an outfitter or search-and-rescue unit is on the scene.

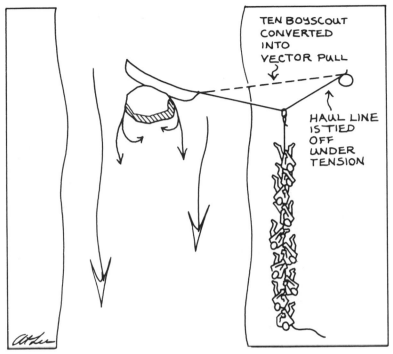

Fig. 6.17. *A vector pull will provide some mechanical advantage and a slight change of direction.*

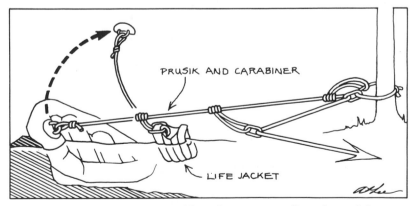

Fig. 6.18. *"Snubber" system on a haul line: if a D-ring pops off, attaching a light weight (a life jacket will do) in the middle of the haul line will cause the line and D-ring to follow the dashed line rather than snapping back directly toward the rescuers.*

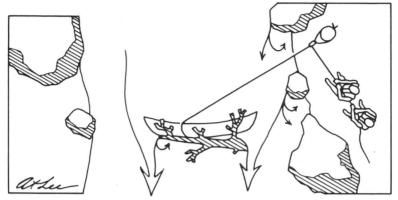

Fig. 6.19. A directional pulley will change the direction of pull but offers no mechanical advantage.

Vector Pull.   Pushing or pulling in the middle of an already taut line will add considerable mechanical advantage, as well as changing the direction of pull slightly. With your ten Boy Scouts, haul as hard as you can on the line and then tie it off under tension. Then tie or clip a second line into the center of the haul line and pull again at a 90-degree angle to the first. This is effective until the haul line is at an angle of 30 degrees or so to its original position. The vector pull can easily be used with other systems and is usually the next thing to try if a direct pull fails. The tighter the line, the more effective the vector pull will be.

Simple Pulley.   Attach a pulley or a carabiner *to the boat,* then run a rope from a shore anchor through the pulley and back to shore (see figure 6.20B). This gives you a 2:1 (theoretical) mechanical advantage, which may be all you need. If you hook a Z-drag (see below) to the haul line, it will give you a 6:1 system (figure 6.20E), but this requires more rope to go out to the boat and back. Do not confuse the simple pulley with the directional pulley (figure 6.20A), which has the pulley on shore and the end of the haul line attached to the boat, and gives no mechanical advantage at all.

The Z-Drag.   The haul system most familiar to river veterans is the Z-drag, a pulley system that may be rigged for several degrees of mechanical advantage. Borrowed from rock climbing, the Z-drag is quite flexible and can be set up quickly with a minimum of equipment. The simplest Z-drag gives a theoretical mechanical advantage of 3:1, and the system can be doubled for a theoretical mechanical advantage of 9:1. The Z-drag is quick to set up and is easily integrated with other systems.

The pulleys referred to in this section will usually be carabiners. A real pulley is ideal for rescue work, because of its low friction, but carabiners can and usually are substituted. Carabiners add friction and therefore reduce the efficiency of any pulley system, but they are more convenient to carry than

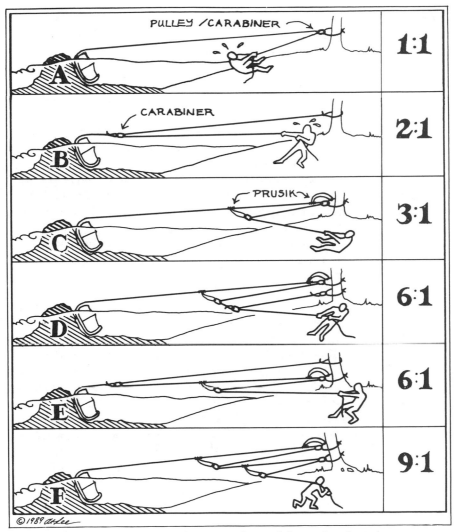

Fig. 6.20. Pulley systems can be rigged in various degrees of theoretical mechanical advantage from 1:1 to 9:1.

pulleys. (For the sake of comparison, the actual mechanical advantage provided by a theoretical 3:1 pulley system would be between 2.5 and 2.7:1 with real pulleys, and about 2:1 with carabiners.)

To set up the Z-drag, first attach the haul line to the pinned boat and figure the angle of pull, then locate an anchor point. A tree or boulder works well, but any secure anchor without sharp edges, such as a car bumper, a root, or a log can be used instead. Remember, though, that the anchor point has to hold the whole load. One group of guides chose a marginal anchor and pulled a boulder over on one of their number. Tie an anchor sling or rope around the anchor point to hold the primary pulley. Run the haul line through the primary pulley at the anchor point, then through a second pulley (the "traveling pulley"), and finally back to the shore.

Attach the traveling pulley to the haul line between the primary pulley and the pinned boat with a prusik (see figure 6.23). A typical Z-drag system uses two prusiks: one is used to secure the traveling pulley to the haul line (the traveling prusik) and the other acts as a brake (the brake prusik; see figure 6.24). You can also use a Bachmann knot, or a Kleimheist knot with webbing, instead of a prusik, but for the sake of clarity we will refer to all cinching knots in this chapter as "prusiks." These knots are useful because they will slide freely on the haul line when loose but will grip under a load. (See the *"Personal Safety Equipment" section* in chapter 2 and appendix D for the knots.) This allows you to slide the traveling pulley easily back down the line to reset it.

The polypropylene ropes often used in river work are rather elastic, so there will be a lot of stretch before the boat moves, and since the traveling pulley moves back toward the anchor point as the rescuers haul on the line, it must be periodically reset farther down the haul line while tension is still maintained on the boat. You can do this with a separate belay line or with a prusik, but using a prusik requires less rope.

Before sliding the loop for the traveling pulley down the haul line, you will have to release the tension on it. Rig the brake prusik to grip in the direction opposite to the braking effect of the traveling-pulley prusik. When the pull on the haul line is relaxed, as when you are resetting the traveling pulley, the brake prusik will grip the haul line and maintain tension on the system. The disadvantage of this system is that the brake prusik may be hard to release when under tension, and there are times when the system is under so much strain that the only thing to do is to release the boat. This may mean cutting the prusik. An alternative to the brake prusik is a separate belay line to maintain tension on the pinned craft while you are resetting the traveling pulley. The brake prusik requires a person to monitor it, since it will become tangled in the anchor pulley when the system pulls forward. A good alternative is the Bachmann knot, which uses a prusik wrapped around a carabiner to cinch on a haul line (see appendix D). This makes an excellent brake, particularly if the rescuers are shorthanded, since the carabiner will not pass through the anchor pulley and has less tendency to tangle.

To multiply the mechanical advantage of the Z-drag system, increase the number of pulleys: a double Z-drag gives a 9:1 theoretical mechanical advantage, and a triple 27:1. Only one brake prusik, attached to the haul line from the boat, is necessary for any of these systems. (For the sake of clarity we have shown each anchor pulley as separate, but in fact a single carabiner can take two lines.)

Although these rigs will increase the pulling force on the haul line, there are some problems. With carabiners as pulleys, friction increases nearly as

Fig. 6.21. This Z-drag is pulling
against the boat pictured in figure 6.9.
It's been set to pull at an angle
to the current.

Fig. 6.22. A prusik knot holds
the traveling pulley to the haul
line. The prusik will grip under
tension but can be slid down
the haul line to reset the pulley
when the tension is released.

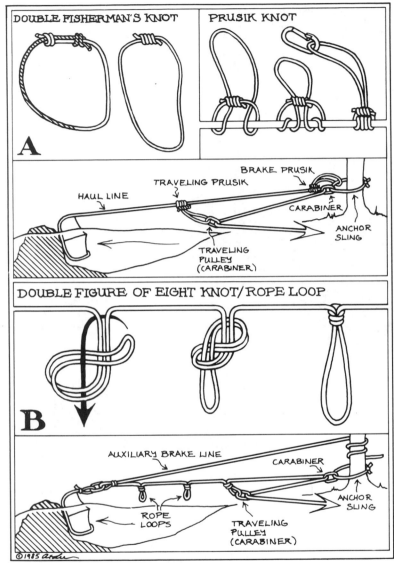

Fig. 6.23. *Two types of simple Z-drag. Type A uses prusik knots to slide down the haul line, while type B uses a series of rope loops. Type B requires a separate belay line to hold the load while the line is reset to the next loop.*

fast as mechanical advantage, and some have doubted whether even a triple Z-drag attains a true 3:1. It also becomes difficult to stop things from getting tangled when you use complicated systems, especially if you are using braided rope. If the mechanical advantage is great, a long pull on one end of the system means a short pull on the other end, and the several pulleys must

Fig. 6.24. The brake pursik, located at the anchor pulley, holds the haul line when tension on the system is released to allow the travelling pulley to be reset. Someone must slide the brake prusik down the line during the hauling or else it will bind in the carabiner. Using a Bachmann knot may overcome this problem.

constantly be reset. Remember, it is sometimes better to try a different angle of pull (or a vector pull) than to increase the pulling power.

The Z-drag seems complicated at first, but with practice it can be set up and used quickly, and it has other practical applications, like pulling out your stuck shuttle car out of the mud on the takeout road.

Piggyback, or "Pig" Rig. The piggyback, or "pig" rig, has been used for some time by search and rescue teams. It gives a greater mechanical advantage than the Z-drag (4:1, as opposed to 3:1) while using the same amount of hardware, although it does use a bit more rope. The big advantage of the pig rig is that is can be switched from one haul line to another without losing tension. If you must pull first on one haul line and then another, this is the system to use.

The pig rig is simply two 2:1 systems set up on top of each other to give a 4:1 pull ratio. To set it up, establish an anchor point and run a haul line out to the boat. Set a belay at the anchor point, using a Münter hitch or descender ring (a simple friction belay will also work). You will need someone to monitor the belay and take up the slack. Then set up a separate 2:1 system (see the simple pulley section above) by anchoring the pig rig's haul line to shore, attaching a pulley to the haul line, and running the haul line through it and back to shore. Now duplicate the system, attaching the next pulley to the haul line on the first system (see figure 6.25). This system completely separates the 4:1 haul system and the belay. The haul system can then be moved to another line if necessary.

If you attach a Z-drag to the first haul line instead of another 2:1 system, you have a 6:1 system.

Sea Anchor Haul System.   This is an ingenious haul system suggested to us by an Alaska wilderness guide. It takes advantage of the force of the current against a boat to provide the pulling force to get the pinned boat off the obstacle. Attach a haul line to the pinned craft, then rig a directional pulley upstream of it to give the correct angle of pull (see figure 6.26). Then run the line to where the sea anchor will be set up. The sea anchor itself can be a swamped open canoe, or a raft in midcurrent. Attach the boat to the haul line with a cradle rig in order to be sure the hull and not the thwarts will take the force. The rescuers will have to maneuver the overturned canoe into the current to load the haul line. If the current on the sea anchor is equal to or greater than the current holding the pinned boat, the boat should come off the obstacle. In particularly stubborn cases it might be possible to use a second sea anchor canoe to add pulling power.

Both the pinned canoe and the sea anchor should have backup belay ropes attached to them to ensure their timely return. Since there is some danger of losing or pinning the canoe serving as the sea anchor, try other methods first.

Conclusion

Les describes an incident in which a little thought about the direction of pull made all the difference: "We had a major problem. One of our rafts was pinned on a rock in the center of the Ocoee River at Broken Nose. All our people were on the right shore. It was the wrong angle of pull, but we figured with all our manpower we ought to be able to muscle it off. We were wrong: a double Z-drag and fourteen people couldn't budge it, and our haul lines were creating a serious hazard for other rafters coming down the river. We took the Z-drag down and sent the rest of the trip on while another guide and I stayed to deal with the raft.

"There were some boulders directly upstream of the pinned raft. A Z-drag rigged from here would still not be at the ideal angle but would be better than what we had previously tried. The boulders didn't have any trees, and I couldn't rig a sling because of the lack of rope. One of the boulders did have a crack and I was able to jam a knot into it to create an attachment point for the anchor pulley. We rigged a simple Z-drag, but still the raft wouldn't move. Finally, with the haul line still under tension, we tried a vector pull by pushing in on it with our hands.

"Imagine our surprise when that raft came off! Especially with just the two of us working on it after fourteen had failed. It showed us what the right angle of pull and some trial and error could do."

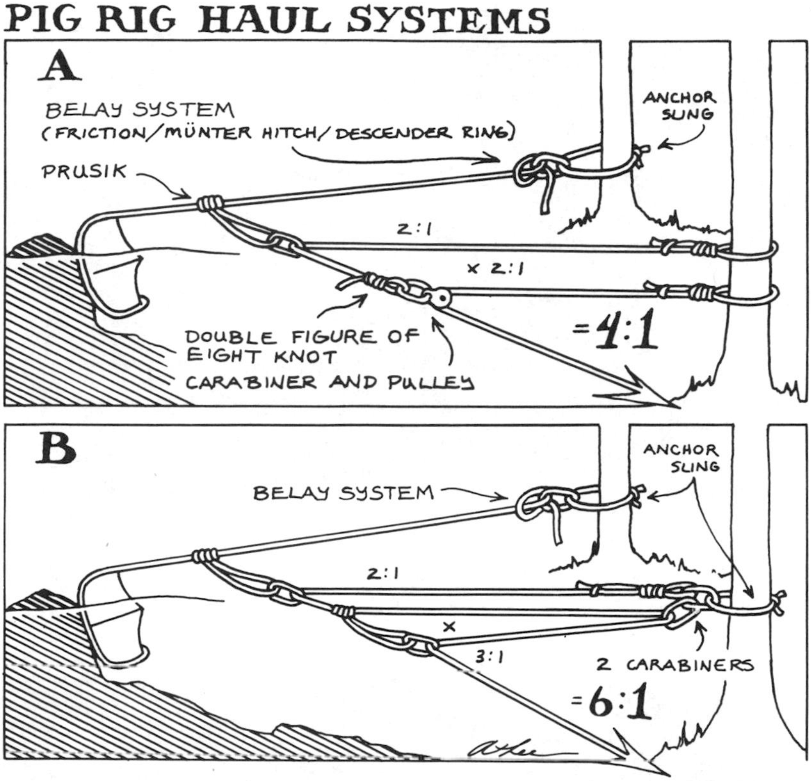

PIG RIG HAUL SYSTEMS

A

BELAY SYSTEM
(FRICTION/MÜNTER HITCH/DESCENDER RING)

ANCHOR SLING

PRUSIK

2:1

x 2:1

= 4:1

DOUBLE FIGURE OF EIGHT KNOT

CARABINER AND PULLEY

B

BELAY SYSTEM

ANCHOR SLING

2:1

x

3:1

2 CARABINERS

= 6:1

Fig. 6.25. The "Pig Rig" haul system. System A works well with two throw bags, while B gives a greater mechanical advantage but requires a longer rope. Either can be detached quickly from the haul line and moved elsewhere.

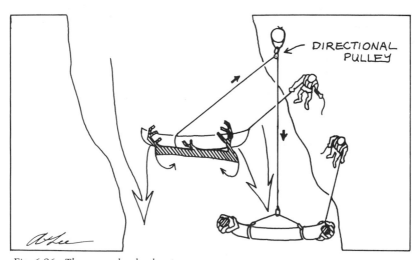

DIRECTIONAL PULLEY

Fig. 6.26. The sea anchor haul system.

Fig. 6.27. Pinned! And solidly, too. Although the guide was unable to prevent the pin, he has gotten his crew safely out of the river.

Fig. 6.28. The rescue crew moves in and begins to set up a Z-drag on some rocks on the center of the river. The haul line is attached to one of the submerged raft's thwarts.

Fig. 6.29. Setting the anchor point on a very strong little tree, they haul away . . .

Fig. 6.30. . . . until the raft comes off.

Fig. 6.31. A raft pinned against a bridge piling on Alaska's Nenana River. This photo makes obvious the equilibrium of forces holding the raft against the piling. (Photo by Jay H. Power)

Fig. 6.32. To unpin the raft shown in figure 6.31, the rescuers pulled up on one end, after first cutting a small hole in the floor and passing a rope around the tube. This upset the force equilibrium enough for the water to pull the boat off. (Photo by Jay H. Power)

Oh to be rescued
from above
On the wings
of a dove
TRADITIONAL

· 7 ·

Vertical Rescue

In a vertical rescue, the rescuer is lowered to the accident site. It is usually a technique of last resort, because of the time required to organize equipment and manpower, and because, like the strong-swimmer rescues, it puts the rescuer in a potentially life-threatening position. A vertical rope rescue also has definite setup limitations. Tyrolean rescues, for example, involve stretching a line across the river (which becomes difficult if the river is over 100 feet wide or if the rope ferry must be done in heavy water) and require anchor points such as trees or boulders at the accident site. Other vertical rescues, such as bridge lowers, require that the structure being used as a base be at or very near the accident site.

Yet there are times when a vertical rescue is best. If the water is too heavy for a Telfer lower or a boat rescue, or if there are no convenient eddies, it may be the only available technique. A low-head dam may have a catwalk above it from which a swimmer might be reached if caught in a hydraulic below. And as we shall see, a simple rope lower can be a very fast and effective rescue method for boats pinned on bridge pilings.

Helicopters may also be used for vertical rescue, but these too must also be considered a last resort, for reasons that will be discussed later in this chapter.

Safety Considerations

We will cover a number of climbing and mountaineering techniques in this chapter. Because of the river orientation of this book, and because there are a number of excellent books already written about them, we have deliberately limited the depth of treatment of these subjects. This chapter is intended to orient rescuers with existing techniques, *not to train them* in using them. Before using any of the techniques involving hanging your body weight from a rope, we strongly recommend that you consult the books on the subject listed in the bibliography, *and* that you get professional training before trying them.

Recreational paddlers should realize that with the ropes they are likely to have with them on the river, safety margins for vertical rescue are likely to be less than ideal. Most technical rope texts, for example, recommend safety ratios as high as 15:1 between the rated strength of the rope and its working strength—for example, a 3/8-inch polypropylene rope with a breaking strength of 2,600 pounds has a working strength of 390 pounds. While enough for a simple bridge lower, this rope would be inadequate for Tyrolean, where the load at the anchors may be several times the rescuer's body weight. This is not to say that the rescuer may not choose to accept the risk in an emergency. We have used 1/2-inch braided polypropylene rope for all the rescues described in this book without problems. Vertical rescues on the river do tend to be somewhat less dangerous than those in climbing, however, since the rescuer is generally operating over water and is rarely more than 30 feet off the surface.

Rappelling

Rappelling is a quick way to reach a victim. It requires only a single person and a minimum of equipment. It does require training, however, and adds another critical thing for the lowered rescuer to manage.

The simplest lower is the body rappel or Dülfer wrap (see figure 7.2). It is easy to set up and requires no extra equipment, but the rescuer can also unwrap easily and fall. You can use a throw bag rope for the Dülfer, but a thicker rope is easier on the body. Pass the rope around an anchor point (such as a tree) and then back down to where you're going. Double the rope if possible: it increases friction and comfort, and you can retrieve the rope by pulling on one end after you reach the bottom. You can, however, use a single rope in a pinch. Run the rope between your legs, around the right thigh to the outside and then diagonally across your chest over the left shoulder, and down across your back to the right side of your waist. The right hand (on the uphill side) guides the rope and the left (downhill) hand controls the rate of descent. Pulling the left (control) hand into your stomach will stop the descent. Wear your life jacket, wetsuit, and gloves, if you have them, to reduce rope burns. The body rappel is not intended to be used as a vertical lower, but rather to assist a person who is climbing down to an inaccessible spot to scout or rescue.

Rescuers can improvise a rappel with little special equipment other than a descender ring or carabiners and an improvised sit harness (see figure 7.3). We do *not* recommend a hanging or "free" rappel with 3/8-inch throw bag rope. Some European life jackets and rescue harnesses (see chapter 2) are already set up for rappelling use. You can use prusiks to ascend back up the rope.

Fig. 7.1. A direct bridge lower on the Ocoee. The victim is given a rope loop and pulled up by simple manpower. A backup belay line would have been a good idea. (Photo by Helen Mary Johnson)

Rappelling can be tricky. Unless you practice it frequently and have the proper equipment, we recommend that you use it only in an emergency if no help is available to set up one of the lowering systems described below. In any case it is a good idea to back up the rappel with a belay line to the rescuer.

Bridge Lowers

A good example of a bridge lower is a rescue at Powerhouse Rapid on the Ocoee River in the fall of 1982. A paddler broached his open canoe on the central bridge support (which has since been removed by the TVA). As the boat wrapped, his left foot became entangled in the webbing of the thigh straps. He could not free himself, although he was able to breathe periodically by doing pull-ups on the gunnel. The force of the water made this difficult, and he was tiring rapidly (see figures 7.20–7.25).

By good fortune, a commercial raft trip was just upstream and quickly responded to the situation. A rescuer tied herself onto a rope and climbed down the iron bridge girders to the victim. The rope was simply run over the bridge railing and the rescuer belayed by fellow guides. The rescuer's first action was to tie off the victim with another line from above to stabilize

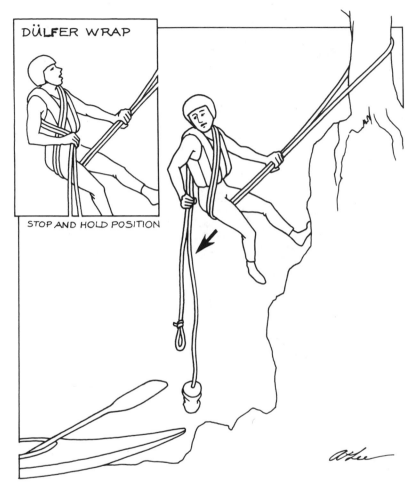

DÜLFER WRAP

STOP AND HOLD POSITION

Fig. 7.2. *The Dülfer wrap, while uncomfortable and somewhat chancy, requires no special equipment other than a rope.*

his position and keep his head out of the water. Next she cut the tangled thigh strap to release the paddler, who by this time was becoming disoriented from fatigue and incipient hypothermia, and moved him onto a small shelf on the lower part of the bridge piling. She then rigged a leg-loop harness for the paddler, and he was pulled to the top of the bridge by sheer manpower. The elapsed time of the rescue was about fifteen minutes.

The rescuers could have rigged a Telfer lower in this case, but a direct vertical lower was faster and more expedient, since there were plenty of people available to haul on the rope. As with most river rescues, speed was the overriding consideration. Fortunately, the rescuers were professional guides used to working together, and this made the organization of the rescue much easier.

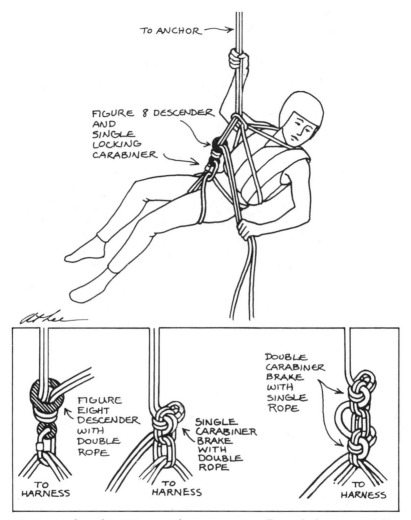

TO ANCHOR

FIGURE 8 DESCENDER
AND
SINGLE
LOCKING
CARABINER

FIGURE
EIGHT
DESCENDER
WITH
DOUBLE
ROPE

TO
HARNESS

SINGLE
CARABINER
BRAKE
WITH
DOUBLE
ROPE

TO
HARNESS

DOUBLE
CARABINER
BRAKE
WITH
SINGLE
ROPE

TO
HARNESS

Fig. 7.3. A descender ring is a simple, easy-to-use rappelling aid. If none is available, rescuers can improvise them as shown with carabiners. Use a double brake with a single rope and vice-versa.

When organizing a bridge lower, consider the following:

- The rescuer to be lowered should be one of the lightest and most athletic of the party. He should have at the least a knife, a helmet, and a life jacket.

- A simple sit harness can be fashioned from a rope or a piece of webbing (figures 7.4, 7.5, 7.6). It is not particularly comfortable, but it is quick to tie and *relatively* secure for the rescuer.

Fig. 7.4. Three steps in tying a simple sit harness. First, make a loop of rope as long as the distance from one shoulder to the opposite outstretched finger, and tie it with a double fisherman's knot.

- A chest harness can be used in addition to a sit harness for increased safety (see figure 7.7). Using the two in combination is safer and more comfortable than is either alone. Some rescue harnesses can be used as chest harnesses, and some life jackets have integral harnesses designed in.

- Position backup safety ropes and boats downstream in case the victim or the rescuer falls in.

- Part of the bridge structure itself, such as a railing, can often be used with a friction belay to make the lower smoother and slower. Wrap the rope around the structure a few times, according to the size and shape of the bridge. One danger with this method is that the rope can be weakened or cut by a sharp edge. If this appears likely, pad the rope or run it through a carabiner tied to the bridge with a sling or piece of rope (see figure 7.8).

- For added safety, back up the main haul line with a belay line on the rescuer. Use a simple friction belay or a Münter hitch (see appendix D) for a brake system.

- If possible, set up the brake system or friction wrap on the downstream side of the bridge. Since accidents almost always happen on

Fig. 7.6. Finally, clip the three loops together, using a locking carabiner or two carabiners with the gates reversed.

Fig. 7.5. Then pull it into three loops, one around each hip and one under the crotch.

the upstream side of the bridge, this gives the rescue team the width of the bridge to work in. If the rope must pass on the upstream side of the bridge, make sure it is padded or run through a slung carabiner to reduce friction.

- Once the victim has been freed, both he and the rescuer must be raised to safety. Unless the patient needs constant attention, he should be raised first. If enough people are available, have them pull on the rope run over the railing, hand over hand, but set up an independent belay in case the main haul line fails. If few people are available, a Münter hitch will work for lowering and for the return belay.

If there are not enough people for a hand-over-hand haul, consider a Z-drag system. An automobile or a winch might also provide the necessary power but must be used carefully.

Tyroleans

We use the term *Tyrolean* to describe any kind of overhead rescue that uses a fixed anchor line stretched across the river. It is a method adapted from the Tyrolean traverse technique used in mountaineering to cross crevasses or to travel from one rock spire to another.

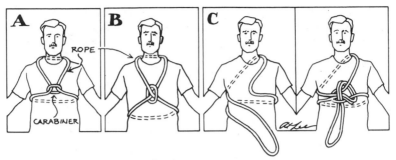

Fig. 7.7. Three types of simple chest harnesses.

Some see the Tyrolean as a system that will magically snatch the victim from the water. This may indeed be the case under some conditions, but for most purposes the Tyrolean is only the first step in a shore-based rescue: its purpose is to get the rescuer near the victim. In most instances, the rescuer will use his position to attach auxiliary lines to the victim or the boat so that the extrication or recovery can take place from shore.

The Tyrolean rescue is dangerous to the rescuer: if the rope or another component breaks, or if an anchor point fails, it means a fall onto the rocks or into the water. Even if the water cushions the fall the rescuer may still become entangled in the ropes. Because of the danger to the rescuer, the time required to set it up, and the amount of equipment and manpower involved, the Tyrolean is another technique of last resort and should be considered only when other methods have failed or are not feasible. In fact, we recommend that you use the Tyrolean *only* if you have had expert instruction in the theory—something there is no room for in this book—and a fair amount of practice in its application.

Professional rescuers have the luxury of sewn sit harnesses, steel cables, winches, and various other tools of the trade. Recreational paddlers will have only those pieces of rescue gear they normally carry with them, which again emphasizes the importance of having every paddler carry a rope and some basic rescue gear. Tyroleans, more than any of the techniques mentioned so far, use a lot of rope, and since the safety of the rescuer rides on it, the quality and strength of the rope is more critical here than in any other application.

Here are some general considerations for using Tyroleans:

- The safety of the rescuer should be a primary concern. Consider the consequences of failure; if you have enough rope, double your anchor lines and use a separate belay for the rescuer, if ·possible, so that he can be brought to shore if the anchor line fails. Position backup safety ropes and boats downstream in case the rescuer goes in or the victim is freed suddenly.

Fig. 7.8. The bridge lower. The rescuer uses the sit harness shown in figures 7.4, 5 and 6. The lowering rope is run through a slung pulley (actually two carabiners with the gates reversed) on the bridge structure. She is lowered by running the rope around the bridge railing to provide enough friction for a smooth descent. Ideally there should be a backup belay rope. The rescuer carries an auxiliary line with her.

- The quality of the rope you use for the anchor line is critical. The safety of the rescuer depends on it. It should be of the highest possible quality and should not have any splices in it. One-half-inch or larger nylon static rescue rope is ideal but will seldom be available. The 1/2-inch polypropylene rope described in chapter 2 will work, but it stretches a great deal more. The 3/8-inch rope in most throw bags is not suitable.

- Place the anchor line under tension by hand if possible: use a Z-drag only if you cannot place the anchor points high enough to prevent the rope from sagging into the water under the weight of the rescuer. This is because with a Z-drag, the prusik loop (made, you will recall, with 5–7 mm rope) now becomes the weak point of the whole system. If you must use a Z-drag tensioning system, double the brake prusiks and make sure you tie the anchor line so that a failed prusik loop will not send the rescuer into the water (see figure 7.15). If possible, back up the anchor line under tension with a slack anchor line.

• Trees usually make the best anchor points for the anchor line. If you can pass the anchor line over a large branch or through a slung carabiner, you will be able to bring the rope down to ground level, where it can be tensioned and secured by hand. Rather than tying off the rope, it is often a good idea to assign a team member to hold the rope in his hands—after having wrapped it several times around a tree. This makes it easy to release if the rescuer gets into trouble. A knife will do the same thing, of course, but is harder on the rope.

• Operating a Tyrolean, especially climbing up and down a rope ladder, is quite strenuous. The person selected to do this should be light and athletic. He should be equipped with at least a helmet, a life jacket, and a knife.

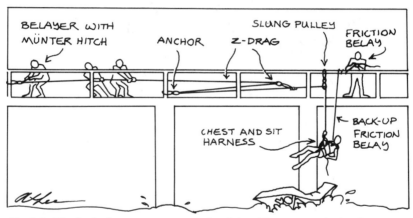

Fig. 7.9. This bridge lower system uses a Z-drag belayed by a Münter hitch. The distance between Z-drag anchor and the slung pulley should be as great as possible in order to avoid having to reset the Z-drag. A backup belay line provides additional security.

• If you have to join two or more ropes for the anchor line, use a double figure-of-eight or a double fisherman's knot (see appendix D). If the rescuer must get his harness carabiner past the knot, the best way to do this is to use a small sling the rescuer can step into to get his weight off the harness carabiner, unclip himself, and clip himself in again past the knot (see figure 7.10). Use a second carabiner and tether to keep the rescuer from falling.

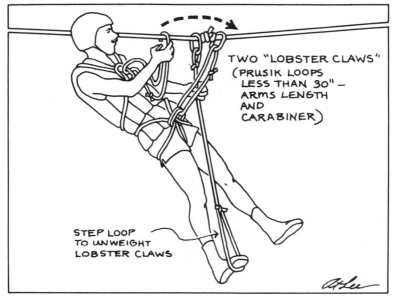

TWO "LOBSTER CLAWS" (PRUSIK LOOPS LESS THAN 30" — ARMS LENGTH AND CARABINER)

STEP LOOP TO UNWEIGHT LOBSTER CLAWS

Fig. 7.10. How to pass a knot on an anchor line. this rescuer uses one lobster claw slipped into a chest harness and another into a sit harness, making for a much more comfortable arrangement than either alone.

There are various types of Tyrolean rescues:

Ranger Crawl.   This is the simplest form of the Tyrolean—and the most dangerous to the rescuer. It is quick to set up and requires a minimum of equipment: a single anchor line upon which the rescuer crawls. Another version, which provides slightly more security, is a double anchor line made with parallel ropes (see figures 7.11 and 7.12). In both cases others in the rescue party slowly release the anchor line(s) to lower the rescuer into position, which means the rescuer must crawl uphill to get back to shore. Use the ranger crawl only when falling in means no more than getting wet.

Sliding Seat.   A simple rope seat attached to a simgle anchor line by two carabiners provides a fairly comfortable way to slide along (figure 7.13). The rescuer slides himself along the anchor line until he reaches the accident site, and the line is then lowered to let him make contact with the victim.

Self-lowering Rescuer System.   After making a harness, the rescuer rigs a Z-drag from the harness to the anchor line (see figure 7.14). The rope is tied to the harness; it passes through one carabiner on the anchor line, down through a carabiner on the harness, up through a second carabiner on the anchor line, and then back down to the rescuer's hands. During the rescue the rescuer adjusts the Z-drag so that he is within arm's reach of the anchor line, holding the loose end of the rope in check with several (four to six) wraps around one thigh. He then pulls himself out over the accident site, hand over hand, with his body weight supported by the harness. When he reaches the accident site he removes the thigh wraps, lowers himself in an action very similar to rappelling, then rewraps the leg to hold himself in place. When he has finished, he can raise himself again, using the Z-drag, and slide back to shore. If he falls into the water the Z-drag should run free. This is a good system if there are only a few rescuers and is very fast to operate.

Fig. 7.11. The ranger crawl—using a single rope.

Fig. 7.12. The ranger crawl—using a double rope.

Shore-based Lowering System.   This is similar to the previous method, except that the lowering is done from shore using manpower, a friction wrap, or a Münter hitch. Attach a carabiner or pulley to the anchor line, holding it in place with a tag line from the opposite shore or by a prusik set on the anchor line (figure 7.15). This system allows the rescuer to concentrate on the victim, although it does require more people to raise the rescuer and return him to shore.

Rope Ladder Rescue.   Probably the most versatile of the Tyroleans, this version includes a rope ladder for the rescuer to climb up and down on (see figure 7.16). The ladder itself is made by tying a series of double figure-of-eight knots. Each loop should be big enough to step into and should overlap the next one (figure 7.17). The rescuer clips directly into the anchor line, pulls himself out over the accident site, clips the ladder into the anchor line, and then climbs down the ladder to the victim. A prusik tied to the anchor line keeps the ladder in position. The rescuer's harness has two short tethers (called lobster claws) with carabiners on each. As he climbs down, the rescuer always keeps one of these clipped into a loop of the ladder. This system might also allow a victim to climb on the ladder and be pulled to shore, or it might also be used to transfer people from one side of the river to another.

Fig. 7.13. The sliding seat is a quick and convenient way to get out over the water, although it is not nearly as flexible as some of the other systems. (Photo by Charlene Swanson)

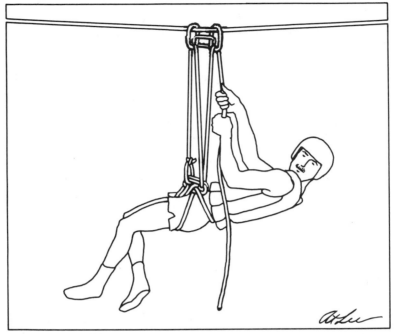

Fig. 7.14. The self-lowering rescuer system.

Helicopters

Helicopters are wonderful tools for rescue and evacuation—if used correctly. Like anything else, however, they are subject to physical laws and have their limitations, and many of the problems that arise in helicopter rescue have stemmed from ignorance of those limitations. Most people, and this includes many rescue professionals, are not familiar with the capabilities of helicopters.

The advantages of the helicopter are mobility and speed. It is sometimes faster than other systems and is especially good for cutting evacuation time to a minimum. It can hover over an accident site where there are no nearby bridge pilings or anchor points and can rescue victims from the middle of rivers too wide for ropes to reach across. Some helicopters, especially military ones, are equipped with powerful winches, which can be used for vertical rescue.

The disadvantages of the helicopter are many and should be carefully considered before use. Helicopters are fast in flight, but they are often slow to respond. Even in areas where they are used frequently, the tasks of getting the required clearances, scrambling the crew, and other administrative details may use time precious to a river rescue. Once the helicopter is on the scene there are often communication problems: unless the group on

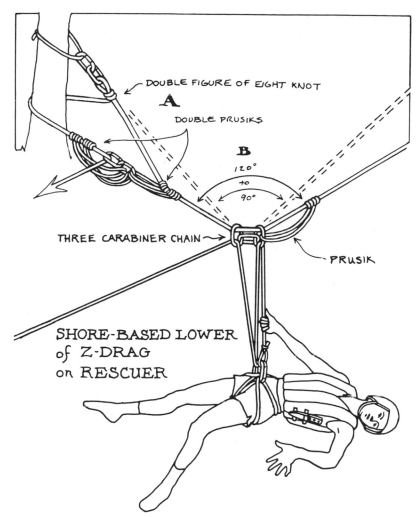

DOUBLE FIGURE OF EIGHT KNOT

A

DOUBLE PRUSIKS

B

120°
to
90°

THREE CARABINER CHAIN →

← PRUSIK

SHORE-BASED LOWER
of Z-DRAG
on RESCUER

Fig. 7.15. The shore-based lowering system. While the anchor line may be tensioned with a Z-drag if necessary to keep the rescuer out of the water, the tensioning system should use doubled prusiks and incorporate a backup (A) in case the prusik breaks. Overtensioning the anchor line puts an acute strain on the anchors and the rope; the angle should be between 90 and 120 degrees (B).

the river has a radio (unlikely) and can talk to the helicopter (even more unlikely), they must use ground-to-air signals, which are slow and inexact (see appendix G). Helicopters also need a lot of room in which to operate, which limits their usefulness in narrow, tree-lined river gorges. If a helicopter snags a rotor and crashes, an already tragic situation becomes much worse. Furthermore, the rotor backwash from a helicopter hovering over a victim can dramatically increase the possibility of hypothermia.

There is an almost universal tendency to overestimate the capabilities of helicopters, which has led rescuers to try to lift water-filled kayaks or to unpin rafts with them. Probably the worst problem with the use of helicopters in river rescue, though, is the temptation to put off rescue attempts "because the chopper will be here any minute." Rescue attempts on the river *must not be put off for any reason*, unless it is absolutely clear that there is no other alternative.

In May 1980 a kayaker became pinned on the upstream side of a boulder on the Kern River in California. He could breathe, but he could not get out of the boat. There were several delays in assessing the situation, and it was nearly half an hour before help was summoned. A deputy sheriff on the scene concluded that a shore-based rescue was too dangerous and prohibited a group of commercial rafters from making any attempts. One guide and a private kayaker did swim out anyway and hold the victim's head up.

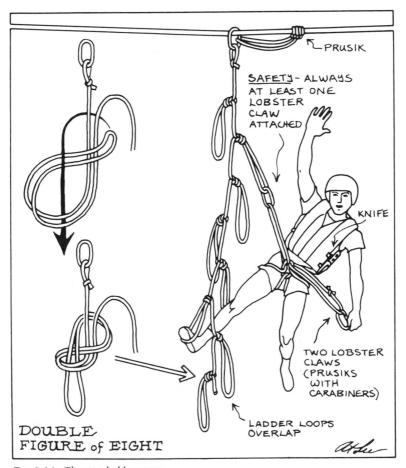

PRUSIK

SAFETY - ALWAYS
AT LEAST ONE
LOBSTER
CLAW
ATTACHED

KNIFE

TWO LOBSTER
CLAWS
(PRUSIKS
WITH
CARABINERS)

DOUBLE
FIGURE of EIGHT

LADDER LOOPS
OVERLAP

Fig. 7.16. The rope ladder rescue.

It was crucial to the deputy's thinking that he had radioed for a helicopter and expected it to be there within fifteen minutes. He did not know that, as Charlie Walbridge comments in the *Best of the River Safety Task Force Newsletter*, "it would take 25 minutes to get the necessary clearances and 35 minutes to scramble the crew before the 15 minute flight could commence." Nor could he communicate with the helicopter's radio, which was on a military frequency.

What followed was a near tragedy. When the helicopter arrived the victim was nearly hypothermic, having been in the water nearly two and a half hours. The helicopter had been called one and a half hours before. The helicopter lowered a rescue collar to the victim, who was still in his kayak, and tried to lift both to the shore, but the helicopter lost lift and almost crashed in the process. Fortunately, in spite of this and more bungling in treatment and evacuation, the injured kayaker escaped from both accident and rescue with only minor bruises.

Walbridge comments that "the people in the helicopter had no idea how much water was in the kayak, or if they had enough lift to do the job, much less if this could be done without injuring the victim." He concludes that "river rescues are not like other kinds. Time works against you and a helicopter is, at best, a back-up."

A similar incident in New Zealand was described to us by our friend Bob Karls, who was working for a commercial rafting outfit there at the time. One of the outfitter's rafts was pinned on a rock on the Shotover River. Despite Bob's offers to set up a Z-drag, the outfitter decided to use a helicopter to unpin the raft. "They use helicopters for everything down there," says Bob, "and they didn't see why they couldn't use it for this."

Fig. 7.17. When making a rope ladder, be sure to tie the loops close enough together. This is a good way to measure the distance.

The outfitter tied the ropes from the helicopter to the raft's D-rings (in spite of Bob's advice to tie them to the thwarts), and the chopper began pulling. "Just as it looked as if the raft might move," Bob recalls, "several of the D-rings popped loose. The ropes to them were stretched like rubber bands, and they jerked the metal D-rings and ropes right into the rotor blades. And I was right under it." By a miracle the helicopter managed to force land without crashing.

The lesson of these incidents is clear: communications, capabilities, and time must all be considered. Does this mean that helicopters should never be used? No. Helicopters are routinely used in the Grand Canyon for evacuation, and the following incident on the Cheat River in West Virginia (reported in the *Best of the River Safety Task Force Newsletter*) shows how they may be used to advantage.

An outfitter's raft flipped on the Cheat at high water. Everyone was rescued except one person, who was stranded on a midstream rock. The river was already beyond the "safe" level for trips and rising. The victim was shaken, and although the outfitter was able to get a kayak over to the rock a huge strainer downstream made the ferry a real risk for a raft. The river was too wide and swift for a Telfer or Tyrolean system, but it was relatively unobstructed. The local rescue squad called a helicopter, which was able to execute a single skid landing on the rock and pick up the victim. In this case the helicopter, which was already in the area, was the best choice.

Helicopter Evacuation

On the whole, helicopters are better used for evacuation, when their speed may be used to get a patient to a hospital quickly, than for rescue. However, even if a helicopter has been called, the rescue and evacuation should proceed as if it were not available. If the helicopter is not needed in the rescue, the rescuers should look for a suitable landing zone for an evacuation. It is much safer, unless the patient's injury is so serious that he can't be moved, to use a proper landing area than to force the pilot into making a dangerous pickup at the accident site.

Communication with the helicopter, as already mentioned, can be a problem, and radios will seldom be available. Several pilots have told us that the best way to get their attention is with a signal mirror, which works even on cloudy days. Other ways to mark the accident site include pocket flares, smoky fires, and waving brightly colored clothing.

The Landing Zone. Set up the landing zone in a flat, clear space with no obstructions around it. Telephone wires or power lines are a special hazard, since they are hard for the pilot to see. An isolated knob or hill is ideal. The landing area should be flat, however, since helicopters cannot land on a slope much greater than 8–10 degrees. A landing zone for the standard UH-1 "Huey" series helicopter should be a minimum of thirty-five paces wide. A pilot can set a helicopter down in a circular area this size, but he will find it difficult to take off or turn around. The landing zone should therefore be three or four times as long as it is wide, and the long axis should face into the wind (see figure 7.19). If there are obstacles like trees and power lines at the end of the "runway," this distance must be greater. Although helicopters *can* take off and land vertically, it is much easier for them to take off into the wind, just as it is for airplanes. Clear the landing zone of all loose debris and brush, leaving no obstacles higher than one foot. Mark it clearly, and if possible arrange for some indication of the direction of the wind. Paddle jackets or brightly colored clothing laid in a T or H pattern will serve as markers, but you will have to stake or weigh them down to keep them from blowing away. Indicate wind direction with smoke or a streamer made from clothing or by standing with your back to the wind and holding your arms forward.

Fig. 7.18. A modern medical evacuation helicopter. Helicopters like this can dramatically cut evacuation time. They are much better suited to this task than that of actual rescue.

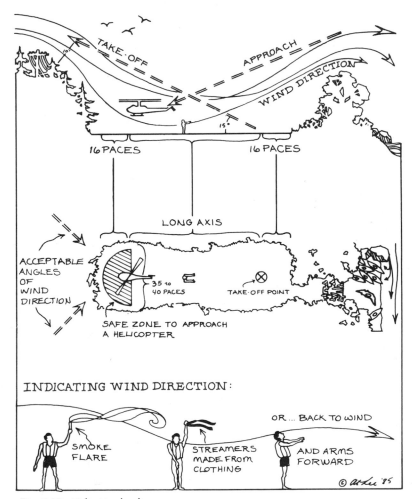

TAKE-OFF

APPROACH

WIND DIRECTION

16 PACES

16 PACES

LONG AXIS

ACCEPTABLE
ANGLES
OF
WIND
DIRECTION

35 to
40 PACES

TAKE-OFF POINT

SAFE ZONE TO APPROACH
A HELICOPTER

INDICATING WIND DIRECTION :

OR ... BACK TO WIND

SMOKE
FLARE

STREAMERS
MADE FROM
CLOTHING

AND ARMS
FORWARD

© atlee '85

Fig. 7.19. Helicopter landing zone.

Evacuation Techniques. Do not rush out to the helicopter when it lands: the pilot may want to move it around first. Instead, make sure you have the attention of the pilot and wait until he indicates he's ready. Approach the helicopter *only* from the front or side—stay away from the tail rotor. If the ground slopes, approach from the downhill side only and duck as you pass under the arc of the rotors. Once you are at the helicopter, a crew member will instruct you where to put the patient. If it is a medivac ship, there will be a doctor or EMT aboard; if not, a first aider should accompany the patient to the hospital, if there is room on the aircraft.

Fig. 7.20. Ocoee Bridge rescue, October 1982. John Norton, an Atlanta canoeist, was rescued by Karen Berry and a group of guides from High Country, an Atlanta-based outfitter. Norton's left foot became entangled in the thigh strap webbing of his canoe as it broached on the bridge piling at Powerhouse Rapid. Norton could breathe only by pulling up on the gunnels. (Photo by Jeff Ward)

Fig. 7.21. The rescuers first attempted to free Norton by lowering a rope to him. When this failed they lowered Berry to the broached canoe. (Photo by Jeff Ward)

Fig. 7.22. First, Berry tied a stabilization line to Norton's wrist, to ensure that his head would remain above water.

Fig. 7.23. Then she cut the thigh strap, releasing Norton . . .

Fig. 7.24.   . . . who was then pulled up on a shelf of the bridge piling in the eddy behind his pinned canoe.

Fig. 7.25. Finally, Berry rigged a sit harness for Norton, who was then raised by simple manpower.

Conclusion

Vertical rescues are a specialized branch of river rescue. They are more dangerous than other kinds, and because they use techniques not familiar to most river runners, they are more likely to require special training and equipment. Generally, except for simple bridge lowers, they should be considered last.

Helicopters can also be used for vertical rescue but are usually better employed for evacuation. Tim Setnicka, who has worked extensively with rescue helicopters in Yosemite National Park, reminds us in *Wilderness Search and Rescue* (Boston: Appalachian Mountain Club Books, 1980) that rescuers "must always consider the negative impact of any one of these factors: bad weather, malfunction, darkness. We therefore want to stay *helicopter independent* in SAR planning and thinking, in spite of the seductiveness of constant reliance on helo support."

There is no right or wrong way to perform a rescue. What matters is whether it is successful.

LES BECHDEL

· 8 ·

Organization for Rescue

The moment of rescue—from the time the need for rescue is recognized until it actually begins—is critical. The most important part of that time is devoted to the organization of the rescue. Because of the very limited time available—a minute or less in a "head-down" pin—organization and timing are vital.

The rescue leader must take charge of the situation *immediately*, assigning responsibilities and directing rescue efforts. If the crisis should involve the trip leader, the leadership role must be assumed by the most experienced paddler in the group. Reaction time is critical: seconds and tenths of seconds count. This is no place for arguments or democratic discussions: the directions of the leader must be followed. For these reasons we suggest that an organized group take the following steps. We realize that some will condemn us as safety fanatics because we are trying to organize a very individualistic sport, but because of the shortness of time available in most rescues there is no substitute for organization and leadership.

The Rescue Process

What factors should you consider when organizing a rescue? You must first assess the situation, communicate the problem, determine the best method of rescue, and organize the rescue. Let's look at each factor in turn:

Assess the Situation

- Where is the victim? Is he entrapped? Does he have a means of self-rescue?
- Can the victim breathe? Is it a "head-up" or "head-down" entrapment?

- How many people are involved? Where are they? What are their skills? Are there other people nearby who can help or go for help?

- Can the situation get worse? How? Can the boat shift? Is the water rising? Is hypothermia a consideration? Can you stabilize the situation until a method of rescue can be worked out?

- How much time do you have? Consider the time left for the victim, the time for rescue, the hours of daylight remaining, and the time needed to summon help.

Communicate the Problem

- To the victim. What is the rescue plan? Can the victim be talked into a reasonable means of self-rescue? The person being rescued will need assurance and will certainly want to know what is being done to help.

- To others in your party and to other parties on the river as quickly as possible, so that everyone knows what the problem is.

- To outside resources, such as a dam keeper or emergency medical services.

Determine the Best Method of Rescue

- Consider the mnemonic *RETHROG*. Can you *RE*ach the victim for a contact rescue? Can you *TH*row a rope to him? Can you *RO*w or paddle to him for a boat-based rescue? Can you *G*o to him with a swimming rescue?

- Consider the time available to set up and use the rescue system. This is vital if the victim cannot breathe or is in extreme danger.

- What danger will each method pose to the rescuers? This is a question too often overlooked. A reasonable risk might be accepted to save a life, but the safety of the rescuers must come even before that of the victim.

- How many people will be needed? With some methods, untrained bystanders can assist.

- How much equipment is required? Some otherwise desirable method may have to be eliminated if critical hardware is not available.

- Can different methods be used concurrently or as a backup? A quick-to-use method like a boat-based rescue can be tried first while another team readies a slower method like Telfer (see figure 8.2).

Fig. 8.1. Rescue team organization is vital for success. Here the rescue leader controls the efforts of two rope teams during a snag tag exercise.

Fig. 8.2. When possible, combine rescue systems. Here a group of rafters recovers one of their number after a spill. They are backed up by a chase boat and a rope farther downstream.

Organize the Rescue

- Appoint individuals to rescue teams if enough people are available. Designate team leaders and tasks. In small groups each paddler will form a team of one.

- The most important thing is to stabilize the patient's condition and start the extrication. The most skilled paddlers and river-wise people should be appointed to the extrication team.

- While the extrication is in progress, prepare for first aid, CPR, and hypothermia treatment as necessary.

- Send for help. Notify local search-and-rescue teams. Prepare for ambulance pickup at the nearest road. If on a dam-controlled river, notify the authorities to shut off water. Call the nearest hospital and give a description of the injuries (see Chapter 9 for the recommended format) so that proper medical facilities can be made ready.

That's a lot to think about, isn't it? How much time do you have to get going? Because of the life-threatening nature of many river emergencies, you must be able to begin the rescue *within fifteen seconds* of the time of the accident. Experience, river sense, and presence of mind count for a lot here: if you have been following the course of events leading up to the accident and automatically analyzing them (the "what if" factor), you should be propelled into action almost instinctively. And though we cannot over-emphasize the importance of time in a river rescue, there is no substitute for the moment of reflection before starting: it is no rescue at all to hurry into an ill-considered attempt that endangers the lives of the rescuers and is doomed to failure because of poor and hasty organization.

Leadership

As a rescue leader you must concern yourself with clear, unemotional thinking. This isn't always easy, particularly if the safety of a friend is involved. If at all possible, you should not become directly involved with any of the individual tasks of the rescue. It is important to have someone who can oversee the whole operation and not get too involved in any one problem. Obviously there will be times when you can't do this; you may be the only one qualified in a certain skill, for example. Remember that your duties as a rescue leader are to *observe, organize, and direct* the efforts of the entire rescue team.

Rescue Priorities

One of the most important factors on the river is always time—the time it takes to set up and use a rescue system and the time a victim may have left. Almost inevitably, time must be traded off against the danger to which a rescuer must be exposed. If the victim's remaining time is measured in minutes or even seconds, a rescuer may be prepared to accept greater danger to himself in order to save a life. But this trade-off must be carefully considered and the attempt skillfully made, with all possible safety precautions taken for the rescuer, or he can end up as another victim.

The rescuers' most important priorities are as follows: First, they must be able to rescue themselves, and not to commit themselves to a rescue unless they can reasonably assure their own safety. Second, they must be able to back each other up and rescue each other. Third, they must rescue the victim. Unfortunately, there may be times when a rescue cannot be attempted because it is too dangerous for the rescuers. Generally, if the situation is immediately life threatening, the fastest system consistent with the rescuer's safety must be used, with safer but slower systems as backups; if people must be rescued but are not in immediate danger, slower and safer systems should be used; if only equipment is involved, choose the safest system for the rescuers.

System Selection

Rescue systems vary greatly in effectiveness, speed, safety for the rescuers, and resource use. What is effective and appropriate in one situation may be useless in another (for example, the most expert chase boater is of little use in a vertical pin rescue). When selecting a system, consider the three S's: safety, speed, and simplicity.

1. *Safety:* How safe is it for the rescuers? The safest place for the rescuer is on the shore, the next safest in a boat, and the least safe is swimming in the water with the victim. Safety must sometimes be balanced with speed, but the safety of the rescuers must be the first consideration.

2. *Speed:* How long does it take to set up? Throw ropes and chase boats are usually the quickest to employ; strong-swimmer and tag lines are next; then tag lines and mechanical rescues; then Telfer lowers; and Tyroleans take the longest.

3. *Simplicity:* How many people does it require? How much equipment is needed? Use the simplest systems first: they are faster to set up and have less to go wrong. Use more complex systems for backups.

The choice of the correct system is an important one, and will often weigh heavily on the minds of the rescuers. When selecting the correct system, consider the following characteristics:

Throwing Rescues and Tag Lines. These are safest for the rescuers, require little special equipment, and are quick to set up. They require minimal training in rope use and safety.

Chase Boat. It is quick to react and set up and requires little special equipment, but is less safe for the rescuer and requires paddling ability equal to the situation.

Telfer Lower. It is less safe for rescuers but requires little paddling ability. It requires practice for quick setup and is slower than above methods to employ. Telfers require a fair amount of specialized equipment (ropes, carabiners, and so forth) as well as organization, leadership, and manpower.

Strong-Swimmer Rescues and Contact Rescues in General. Least safe for rescuers but very quick to employ in situations in which rope throws and chase boats are not appropriate, such as pins and broaches. Minimal equipment and manpower are needed.

Tyrolean. Slow to set up and employ, and least safe for the rescuer (who is over the river), it requires specialized equipment and training, leadership, and manpower.

Team Organization

It would be impossible to set out here exactly what organization you will use for a rescue. Each rescue is different, and the equipment, experience, and numbers of people available will vary greatly. One primary goal is to make the best use of all available manpower, and the most effective way to do this is to organize people into teams. Our intention here is to provide a guide to all the teams (or functions, if you prefer) that you might have in an ideal situation. In a small group some or all of these team functions will be performed by individuals, and in some cases one person may have to perform them all.

The organizing should be done by the rescue leader, except when he is deeply involved in an extrication or other rescue task (for which he might be the only one qualified), or in the case of a small group of experienced paddlers who, thanks to experience and instinct, react instantly (see figure 8.3). If for any reason the trip leader cannot organize the rescue, someone else, preferably the next most experienced person, must take over.

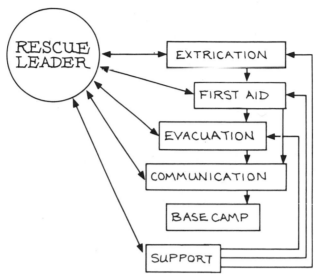

Fig. 8.3. Rescue organization.

The following teams are usually needed:

- *Extrication team.* Most needed in pin or entrapment, more often than not this team is not appointed at all but consists of the people nearest to the scene of the accident. Because speed and efficiency are critical, this team should be composed of the most experienced and water-wise paddlers.

- *First aid team.* The "aid" team prepares to treat the patient while the extrication is going on. It should include medically the best-trained people present and is responsible for the treatment of the patient. The aid team must determine where CPR will be performed, who will do the compressions and who the breathing, what first aid is needed and where, and whether a litter or backboard is necessary.

- *Evacuation team.* The "evac" team coordinates with the aid team to determine the best method of evacuation, then selects the evacuation route. The team also constructs or locates litters or backboards and perform the evacuation.

- *Communications team.* The "commo" team goes for help. After receiving instructions from the trip leader, the team will go by the best means available (foot, paddling, hitchhiking) to make contact with outside agencies such as search-and-rescue teams, ambulances, and hospitals. Contingency plans should be discussed *before* leaving the other teams. It is a good idea, if possible, to send out people in pairs, in case one is injured.

- *Support team.* The support team takes care of everything else. Someone must look after the other group members, who may be having their own problems with shock, grief, or hypothermia. If the group needs to keep moving down the river or to split up who will be the new leader? The support team may have to prepare a fire, a meal, or a campsite. If the accident happened near a road someone will need to control curious onlookers. One member of the support team should be upstream of the accident site to warn other paddlers; another should stand downstream with a backup rope for the extrication team. Finally, someone should be taking notes and, if possible, photographs so that a record of the incident can be made.

- *Base camp.* It may be necessary to set up a base camp with someone to receive and coordinate information and resources, comfort friends and relatives as needed, provide continued support with food and clothing, and deal with the media. Often this function is performed by the commo team at the takeout or put-in.

If the First Attempt Fails

What happens when the first attempt fails? Obviously you can't just give up while you have the means in your power to rescue someone.

If enough people are available, some should be working on an alternative method of rescue while the primary method is being tried. For instance, if a paddler is pinned in a boat in midstream, you might first try sending a rescue team out in a canoe or raft. While this is being done, a second team can be stretching a rope across the river to prepare for a Telfer lower or a Tyrolean rescue.

Reassess the situation, using the same criteria you did the first time. Don't give up! Was there something you missed? Has the situation changed? Are there other alternative methods you haven't considered? Solicit suggestions from others. Are the rescuers getting tired or otherwise endangering themselves? In your concern for the victim do not ignore the effects of hypothermia or shock on the rescue party. Has someone been sent to notify others, such as a search-and-rescue team, who might have equipment you don't have?

Keep trying, and keep thinking. Keep the rescuers safe, but don't give up until the situation is clearly hopeless. Remember that apparent victims of drowning have been revived after over half an hour's immersion in cold water.

Liability

In these days of the "sue everybody" society, the question of liability frequently comes up. Unfortunately, there is lot of misinformation about it, even in the legal community. In the simplest terms, you are liable to a person when, through fault or omission, you cause injury to that person or his property. After that it gets complicated, and discussions of this subject have filled many law books.

What happens when you see someone in trouble on the river? Are you under an obligation to help? And what happens when you do? Many states have "Good Samaritan" laws, which protect a would-be rescuer who acts in good faith. Some even make it a crime *not* to render aid. What's good faith? It just means that you are really trying to do the right thing within the limits of your knowledge and capabilities. You are not expected to endanger yourself or attempt the impossible.

Still, it is impossible to have a lawyer on every trip, and in some cases the river you're on may even be the border of two states with different liability laws. As a practical matter, there are too many things to think about during a rescue—you don't need to add liability to the list. Your knowledge will protect you; if you know river rescue and first aid, use good judgment, and try to prevent accidents before they happen, your chances of being sued as a private boater are very slight.

The Media

If the accident is near a road, you may be visited by members of the media. This might mean anything from a part-time newspaper reporter to a full "action news team" with cameras, lights, and sound. Media people can be distracting and sometimes obnoxious, but they have a right to be there *as long as they don't interfere with the rescue or evacuation*. If the sheriff or a search-and-rescue outfit is on the scene, one of them will usually take care of media relations. If not, one of your group will have to do it.

Probably the worst thing you can do is to try to keep the media away altogether and refuse to comment. This will invariably raise suspicion that you are trying to hide something. The best policy is to give a general statement ("Yes, there's been an accident here, and we're in the process of attempting to rescue that fellow over there"). Most reporters respect this and will be satisfied with the basic facts. The details can wait for later.

You are well within your rights to keep reporters and bystanders out of the immediate rescue and evacuation work area. A rope run around the work area works well to define it.

There is one thing, however, that you should *never* tell any reporter: the name of the victim, particularly if he is dead or seriously injured. That information is not to be made public until the victim's next of kin can be notified. Notification is the job of a clergyman or a close friend and is not the sort of thing for someone to hear about first on the five o'clock news.

Thinking the Unthinkable—The Failed Rescue

In a book, all rescue attempts can be successful, but in real life you must be prepred to deal with those that fail. An unsuccessful rescue means someone is dead. Death is not a pleasant thing to think about, but it's something that you must consider as a logical extension of organizing for rescue.

As we have said, the rescuers must keep trying to save or revive the victim until the situation is clearly hopeless. What then? If there is no doubt that the victim is beyond help, a decision must be made as to whether to continue efforts to recover the body. Because of the emotional attachment of people in the rescue party to the victim, this may be a hard decision to make, but you should continue recovery efforts only if they are not compromising the safety of the rescuers.

Consider the condition of the rescuers. They are almost certainly tired and emotionally upset by what has happened. Is the party near a road or takeout? How much daylight is left? Should the party continue or abandon the trip? The safety of the living must come first. If the group is near a road or town and recovery attempts have been fruitless, it may be better to leave the attempt to a sheriff's department or a search-and-rescue unit. If you are on a multiday wilderness trip, the victim may have to be left for a later search party. It is well known among mountaineers that a party will tend to abandon an expedition after a death, regardless of the actual difficulties. Certainly the death of a companion affects any undertaking, but the risks and rewards of continuing must be evaluated realistically.

Suppose the rescue is unsuccessful, and the victim has been recovered. What do you do with a dead person, especially a friend? If all attempts at revival have failed, remove the body to a safe place until you can either evacuate it or arrange for that to be done. If you are in the wilderness and far from help, you may have to bury it, either temporarily or permanently. In either case the grave must be marked.

In most places in the United States a person must be pronounced dead by a civil official, usually a coroner or a medical examiner. The coroner must file a report and, if he thinks the circumstances warrant it, order an investigation. Any death must be reported to the local police department or county sheriff, along with the circumstances. These authorities will want specific information. To be able to provide this information, the people involved in a rescue, whether it involves a fatality or even a near miss, should debrief as a group as soon as possible. It is surprising how quickly people forget details and how subjective impressions of time are. The only way to be sure is to write things down as soon as possible after the event.

Try to specify exactly what happened: who did what and in what order. If possible, take photographs of the accident site, the rescue, the evacuation, and the victim. It may seem morbid to take pictures at a time like this, but they are invaluable in trying to piece together events later. A photograph will not forget details.

Fig. 8.4. Rescues save lives, but sometimes they fail. What would your reactions be to the death or serious injury of one of your party? (Photo by Cindin Carroll/Nantahala Outdoor Center)

Another reason for setting all this down is to pass on the experience, good or bad, to others who might at some time be in a similar situation. Write down a summary of the accident and send it in to the Safety Committee of the American Canoe Association (see Introduction).

Reactions

We have talked about successful and unsuccessful rescues and some of the administrative considerations involved in both, but what really happens in your mind when there is a fatal accident on the river?

At the beginning of the emergency there is faith, a certainty that the victim will be saved. This is replaced by disbelief that the accident is really happening, and then by hope that a miracle will occur. Inevitably, there is the realization that the accident actually has happened and the anger and frustration that go with that realization. This is often coupled with a strong sense of personal guilt, regardless of the circumstances. Finally, there is the acceptance of death, which leaves a numbing feeling that lasts for some time.

As a conclusion to this chapter, here is Les describing some of his feelings after a drowning death on the Bío-Bío River in Chile:

"It was to be my last trip on the Bío Bío. After four seasons there I had come to love the beauty of this rugged river and its whitewater. We were running Lost Yak rapid and my raft was first. We took on a lot of water and went through the next rapid, Lava South, as well. As I returned to Lost Yak on foot another raft was coming through, and then I saw Ted in the water away from the raft. Because of the width of the river we were unable to use safety ropes to reach him, but John approached him in a kayak. Ted grabbed the boat, and they began to struggle toward shore. I had *faith* in John's ability, but a lot of cold, fast Class IV water lay between them and safety.

"My mind flashed back to a similar incident two years before [the rescue described in the Prologue]: we were at the bottom of Lava South, and a person from another company, who had fallen out of his raft in Lost Yak, was forced to swim through Lava South. That time we were lucky to be in the right place at the right time.

"Ted died only a few feet from shore. Caught under a rock, he was still clutching the kayak's grab loop. *Disbelief.* This can't be happening. I watched helplessly from the opposite shore as Ted disappeared facedown into Lava South. John had lost his paddle in the struggle to free Ted and was trying to follow him on foot. All our other rescue attempts, some foolish and some brave, ended without success.

"Somewhere during all this my hopes crashed. *Frustration* had been growing during the pursuit of Ted's body and it ended in *anger*. It wasn't fair. We had done everything by the book, taken every precaution. He was an experienced paddler. I had to turn my anger and despair into something else. We had to start thinking about ourselves. As I walked back to the rest of the group, waves of *guilt* washed over me. We should have portaged around Lost Yak. I should have been able to do something to save Ted. It was my fault that he was here. And now he was dead.

"Getting the group together that night wasn't easy. Each of us had his own way of dealing with the grief. We didn't know whether to quit or go on. We knew we had to get out of the canyon; after that we would take it one day at a time. We finished the trip and took out four days later at Santa Barbara. The authorities found the body the next day.

"My trip lasted longer. We sent Ted's body back to West Virginia, and it was there at his funeral that I *accepted* the reality of his death. His mother asked me if the river was beautiful and I said that it was. She said, 'At least he died doing something he loved the most . . . paddling whitewater on a beautiful river.' "

Imbecilli fluvidique inter vana constitimus. (We are weak, watery beings, standing in the midst of uncertainties.)

SENECA

· 9 ·
Patient Care and Evacuation Techniques

"We had put together a good rescue, and I was congratulating myself as we neared the end of the evacuation trail. Then, as we slid the litter over a fallen tree, our patient cut his finger. His respiration became shallow, he wouldn't respond to our comments, and he had poor color. This insignificant injury to his finger sent him over the threshold of tolerance, and he began losing the stoic control he had been exercising. With great effort he brought himself back, but it was close.

"He had broken his leg in Corkscrew Rapid on the Chattooga. The rescue was quick, and minutes later we had him on shore with an air splint in place. He was obviously in pain but was staying in control. We got the emergency backboard, and within half an hour we were carrying him down the rocky banks of the river. What we failed to do was to instruct our patient on how to protect himself while being transported in a litter. When we slid him over the log we hadn't noticed that he was gripping the edge of the litter. It was another lesson in patient care."

Until this point our concern has been with rescuing the victim of an accident. When rescued, however, a victim becomes a patient, and in this chapter we will be dealing with the person who is now your patient. It is not our intent to cover general first aid procedures, but we do want to highlight some thoughts on postrescue care that should concern any river rescuer.

Anyone involved with outdoor sports should have some form of first aid training. Outdoorspeople frequently find themselves engaged in an active sport where injury in a wilderness setting is a distinct possibility. Professional help can be hours, days or even weeks away, which means that some training in dealing with medical emergencies is a must. The usual Red Cross/ EMT (emergency medical technician) standards were developed for an "ambulance" context; meaning that the treatment standards and techniques were based on the assumption that advanced medical treatment was twenty minutes or less away. However, treatment in a "wilderness" context (loosely defined as being more than twenty minutes to an hour away from advanced levels of medical treatment) requires some modification of accepted procedures and techniques, as well as some knowledge of conditions not thoroughly covered by conventional first aid training—for example, altitude wilderness evacuations and dislocations.

The National Association for Search and Rescue (NASAR) has developed a series of wilderness medicine training programs that address emergency treatment in the wilderness context, including issues such as prolonged transport, severe environments, and improvised equipment. These programs include Wilderness First Aid, First Responder, and Emergency Medical Technician (EMT-W) (see the Afterword for more on NASAR training programs). Much of this chapter is based on these courses. We urge all paddlers, but especially those who frequent remote areas, to take these courses if possible.

Several traumatic injuries, fortunately, are rare on the river. For the most part paddlers need concern themselves with the "big three": drowning, hypothermia, and shoulder dislocations.

The Initial Contact

At some point in the rescue process you must make hands-on contact with the victim. This is the only way to rescue an unconscious person. But when making direct contact, especially at or near the accident site, you must be wary of the conscious victim: he may be in severe pain or have just experienced a close brush with death. A distraught victim in the water may make a desperate lunge for the rescuer or try to climb on top of him. A victim stranded on boulders in midstream, pinned in a boat, or with his foot entrapped may have been in that position for some time—his actions may be difficult to anticipate.

When approaching a victim it is a good idea to have a rescue plan in mind. Communicate it to him. Tell him exactly what you are doing and planning to do, and what you want him to do. Ask his name. Ask about injuries: "Where does it hurt?" If you are new to the scene, ask if there are others in the party. Try to get as much information about the accident and the patient's condition as you can. If the patient is conscious but not responding to your inquiries, be cautious.

If you have witnessed the accident and know the patient, use his name. Be calm and reassuring. Be honest about the situation, remain positive, and try to inspire trust and confidence. The first few seconds of interaction may make the difference between a patient who remains cool and one who goes off the deep end. A patient's mental condition is critical and should be monitored at all times. Rescuers should be aware of ASR (autonomic stress response, or acute stress reaction), which can easily be confused with shock. As we saw in the opening paragraphs of this chapter, an otherwise insignificant injury or even a seemingly innocuous remark ("God, he looks terrible") overheard by the patient may be enough to trigger ASR, or worse. This is true even of unconscious patients. The patient may then appear "shocky," causing the rescuers to misread the urgency of the situation. Make sure you have properly assessed the patient's physical condition (see below) before you conclude that he is in shock. The patient in the incident described at the beginning of this chapter was in no danger of dying, although he may have appeared so to the rescuers.

If the patient is stationary and out of immediate danger, your primary concern should be to *assess* his condition correctly and *stabilize* it so that it doesn't get worse. We have previously discussed strategies to use in pinning and entrapments, so the emphasis here is on assessing the nature of the patient's injuries and his emotional state. Do not aggravate the patient's condition by hasty, unnecessary movement. First, make a quick survey of the patient's condition. You will need to do this in a systematic way, as if following a pilot's checklist, otherwise you may not know where to begin, or worse, you may forget an important step. We have outlined the process below; the complete NASAR Patient Assessment System is reproduced in appendix J. Neither of these is intended to replace the appropriate courses.

- Survey the scene: Is there *danger* to the rescuer? What was the *mechanism* for the injury?

- Conduct a primary survey, using the ABCD system: Is the **A**irway clear? Is the patient **B**reathing? Is the **C**irculation intact? (Is he bleeding?) Is there a **D**isability from the injury? Be especially careful with patients with a mechanism for cervical spine injury. If there is a problem with any area in the primary survey, you must correct it before continuing.

- Conduct a brief secondary survey of the patient's head, eyes, ears, nose, mouth/throat, neck, chest, abdomen, pelvis, genitalia, legs, arms, back, and buttocks. Look for injuries that might not be obvious on first inspection.

- Check the patient's vital signs: pulse, respiration, and skin color. If you are equipped to do so, take blood pressure and temperature. Note the time and the patient's consciousness and mental status: is he **A**lert; not alert but responds to simple **V**erbal questions; nonverbal but responds to **P**ain; or **U**nconscious?

- If the patient is conscious, get a history, including any allergies, medications and when last taken, any past medical problems that might affect treatment, the time of the last meal, and the patient's recollection of the accident.

- Especially if you are faced with a lengthy evacuation or must communicate with medical support, write down all the above information. This will prevent confusion and allow supporting rescuers to have the right equipment ready. Use the SOAP note format: What are the patient's **S**ubjective complaints? What are your **O**bjective findings? What is your overall **A**ssessment of the situation and anticipated problems? What is your **P**lan for treatment and evacuation?

- Continue to monitor your patient's condition, including vital signs, and note the times. Often a problem will become obvious only after looking at the pattern of a patient's condition over time.

A contact rescue in the water does not offer much time for a survey of the patient's condition. If the victim is conscious you can ask about his injuries; if the victim is unconscious and breathing, stay on the upstream side of him and keep his head above water. In heavy water, position yourself under the patient with his and your feet downstream (see figure 9.1). Hold him in a bear hug while keeping his face close to yours, in order to provide a little extra buoyancy. Once you reach calmer water you can swim the patient to shore by using a cross-chest carry or by grasping his hair or helmet.

Fig. 9.1. For contact rescues in heavy water, use the bear hug (A) to add buoyancy and keep contact with the victim, then use the cross-chest carry (B) in calmer water to swim the victim to shore.

Drowning

The primary threat to a paddler's life is respiratory failure in a fluid environment, or drowning. Drownings can generally be divided into two types: dry and wet. In the dry drowning a spasm of the larynx closes the airway and prevents water from entering the lungs. This probably happens in about 15 percent of the cases. Although the spasm will ultimately relax, persons in this condition have a much better chance of survival with basic life support procedures (that is, CPR), particularly if the victim's metabolism is also slowed because of hypothermia. On the other hand, a wet drowning means that a substantial amount of water has entered the lungs. Water in lung

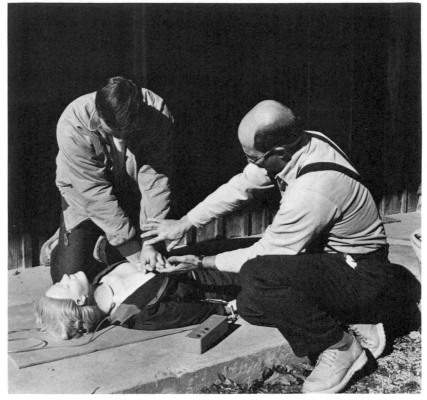

Fig. 9.2. Every paddler should take a course in cardiopulmonary resuscitation (CPR).

tissue causes pulmonary edema and other harmful effects: the effects may be delayed up to twenty-four hours. There have been several cases in which a near-drowning victim has been revived, only to die several hours later in a hospital. Any person revived after a near drowning must be taken to a hospital immediately, no matter how well he or she might feel.

Cardiopulmonary resuscitation, or CPR, is a proven life-saving technique that every whitewater paddler should know. For a drowning victim, the most important thing is to start it as soon as possible, even if this means doing ventilations in the water when you first make contact. Your first step, assuming there is no mechanism for cervical spine injury, will be to open the victim's airway by pulling up on his neck with one hand and pushing down on his forehead with the other. This tilts the head back and may cause the patient to start breathing again on his own. Although you can ventilate a person in the water, you cannot perform adequate chest compressions. However, many drowning victims will simply be in respiratory arrest and will not require chest compressions. For effective chest compressions, get the patient to the nearest hard surface: this could mean boulders in midstream, gear boxes on a loaded raft, or even the hull of a canoe. Do not spend precious moments hauling the victim up a river embankment if you can find a flat place at the water's edge. If you are alone, initiate one-person CPR until help arrives. (For details on CPR, see appendix II.)

Start CPR if the victim has been underwater for less than one hour. After that, most experts agree that CPR has little, if any chance of reviving a drowning victim. After starting CPR, continue until the patient starts breathing on his own, is transferred to a higher medical facility, or *the rescuers are at risk*. If you do not detect a pulse after thirty minutes, further chest compressions have very little chance of producing recovery. Ventilation, however, can be beneficial even if prolonged since a pulse may be present but undetectable.

What does this mean to the rescuer in the field? Do the best possible CPR before attempting to transport the patient: you cannot perform effective chest compressions while moving. In an emergency like this you will feel urgently that you want to get the patient to an ambulance or hospital, but don't jeopardize the quality of your CPR in a rush to evacuate. After half an hour, you may transport the patient while continuing ventilation. In remote areas, when the patient has not responded and no medical assistance is nearby, the safety of the group may outweigh the need to continue ventilation.

If CPR is successful and the patient begins to breathe on his own, rescuers must stand by to restart CPR at any time. Keep the patient warm and quiet, and evacuate him. Under no circumstances allow a paddler who has undergone CPR to get back in his boat. If you are forced to spend the night in the field, the patient's condition should be continuously monitored, preferably by at least two people.

Paddlers should be aware of the mammalian diving reflex (MDR). Sudden immersion into cold water (70 degrees Fahrenheit or less) sometimes triggers an autonomic response that slows the heart rate and concentrates circulation between the brain and heart. All body functions are slowed to a barely discernible point; the body is sustained on the oxygen present in the blood and tissues at the time of immersion. To an observer the victim may appear dead: he has very slow and shallow respiration; weak, slow pulse; fixed, dilated pupils; and clammy, white skin. Victims have been revived without brain damage after being submerged for as long as one hour. Whether it is MDR or hypothermia that is protective, the point is not to give up on rescue efforts or CPR just because four minutes (the old standard of "clinical death") have passed. If the victim is young, the water is cold (below 70 degrees) and clean, and the submersion time is less than one hour, MDR may have occurred and you should start CPR as soon as possible. Acute hypothermia produces similar symptoms.

Hypothermia

Few paddlers die of hypothermia, but it is very often a contributing factor in drowning. Hypothermia occurs when the cold challenge of the environment (that is, low temperature, wet conditions, and wind) overwhelms the body's ability to respond to it and maintain a constant temperature. The body's ability to do this is affected by its size and shape, insulation, percentage of body fat, fluid status, and the available "fuel" stores of glycogen. The body's immediate response to the cold challenge includes reducing the circulation to the shell areas (that is, the extremities and surface areas of the body) and increasing blood flow to the core. The body also produces heat by burning more fuel and by exercise. Shivering is involuntary exercise, as the body tries to generate heat. Subacute hypothermia, often called "mountain" or wind-chill hypothermia, is a long-term process in which the body gradually loses the contest with the cold. The onset is measured in hours or days. Of more concern to the paddler, however, is acute or "immersion" hypothermia, caused by sudden immersion in cold water. This generates a very high cold challenge that can overwhelm the body's response in a matter of minutes. It is characterized by sudden onset and a radical temperature differential between the body's core and shell. Frequently the body's stores of fuel are almost intact. This is often how paddlers drown: the shell (that is, arms and legs) quickly loses strength and coordination, which makes the victim unable to perform even simple self-rescue tasks like swimming or holding a rope.

Hypothermia is usually classified as mild/moderate or severe, depending on whether the body's temperature is over or under 90 degrees Fahrenheit.

The best way to deal with hypothermia is to prevent it. Wear the proper clothing and have the skill to paddle the water you've chosen. Know the warning signs of hypothermia (see appendix I), and take action to keep matters from worsening as soon as you recognize them. Hypothermia affects judgment and coordination and is insidious in its effects. A good example is that of the paddler who swims once and gets cold, then starts missing his roll and swims again and again, becoming colder and more exhausted each time until finally he becomes hypothermic. Keep an eye on people after they swim. If it happens again right away and they are shivering, it is time to suggest a warm-up.

Early recognition of hypothermia is important. Generally a victim will be shivering, uncoordinated, and may experience mild to noticeable changes in mental status. What is the best treatment for hypothermia on the river? One group's recommendation for mild/moderate hypothermia (body temperature above 90 degrees Fahrenheit) is to "feed 'em and beat 'em" (that is, food and exercise). In the early stages the patient can walk, and that's exactly what he should do. Walking will rewarm him and get him away from the probable cause of his hypothermia—the cold water. Consider walking out from the site, but don't let the patient do it alone; hypothermia is notorious for clouding a person's judgment, and people have gotten lost on simple trails because of it. At least one and preferably two people should accompany the patient. An often overlooked treatment is to have the patient replenish his food *and* fluid supplies.

When walking, do not ignore wind chill, rain, and other factors. Several fatalities have occurred when paddlers have tried to walk out in very poor conditions and never made it. If you carry basic survival gear (including matches), it may be better, especially if you can find a protected spot, to try to rewarm a moderately hypothermic patient on the spot while someone goes for help. Build a fire, and if possible get the patient into dry clothes or a sleeping bag. If these aren't available, use extra clothing from other members of the group. Give the patient a warm, nonalcoholic drink. You may also choose to use body heat from the other members of the group in a "human sandwich." Skin-to-skin contact is necessary for this to work. Another solution is to heat moist life jackets in front of a fire and wrap them around the patient, exchanging them for freshly warmed ones as they cool. The more advanced the hypothermia, the less effective field rewarming techniques will be.

Field rewarming is impractical and medically unsound with severe hypothermia (core temperature below 90 degrees). Hypothermia becomes critical here; the body can't rewarm itself without outside help, even in a dry sleeping bag, and there is a danger of cardiac arrest if the patient is suddenly rewarmed or handled roughly. This stage of hypothermia is on the whole easily recognized: the patient is unconscious or has severe mental status changes, and has stopped shivering. To measure body temperatures in this range (below 94 degrees) you will need a special hypothermia thermometer.

Severely hypothermic patients *must* be evacuated to a hospital. Insulate the patient as well as possible to retain remaining body heat (a vapor barrier works well) and handle gently (a hypothermic person's heart is subject to ventricular fibrillation, or uncontrolled beating, if handled roughly). Ventilate the patient if he appears to have stopped breathing, but remember that the body is now in a "metabolic icebox," and pulse and breathing may be barely perceptible. This is a protective response: people have been revived with a core temperature of 64 degrees Fahrenheit and no heartbeat. The use of chest compressions in a hypothermic patient is a controversial question because of the urgent need for evacuation and the danger of ventricular fibrillation. Many experts recommend that rescuers ventilate severe hypothermics as long as possible, and reserve chest compressions for patients who lose pulse during an evacuation. They further recommend that no chest compressions be given if doing so will significantly slow the evacuation or if it puts the rescuers at risk.

Shoulder Dislocations

Whitewater paddling can cause a variety of injuries: broken limbs and noses, sprains, cuts and so on. A common injury, particularly among kayakers, is the dislocated shoulder. A shoulder dislocates when the ball of the upper arm pops forward out of the socket of the shoulder. It is always painful.

Shoulder dislocations are most often caused by poor paddling technique. It typically occurs when a paddler extends his arm away from his body, rotates it rearward on a brace, turns his head in the opposite direction, and receives a jarring blow on the paddle (see figure 9.4). All paddlers should take the time to learn proper paddling technique and methods of avoiding shoulder dislocations.

Fig. 9.3. The dislocated shoulder is especially common among kayakers.

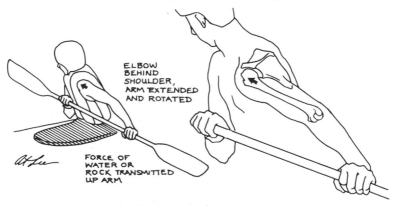

ELBOW BEHIND SHOULDER, ARM EXTENDED AND ROTATED

FORCE OF WATER OR ROCK TRANSMITTED UP ARM

Fig. 9.4. This is how a shoulder dislocation happens.

First aid field treatment is to put a sling on the arm and then tie a swath bandage around the body to keep the arm immobilized. The patient should be evacuated, and although he can usually walk he should not be sent out alone. If evacuation time is under three hours the shoulder probably should be "reduced" (put back in place) by a doctor. However, paddlers venturing into remote areas may want to learn methods of reducing a shoulder dislocation. This is especially true of those who have suffered a dislocation in the past, since they are more likely to have it happen again. Though methods of reducing shoulders in the field are beyond the scope of this book, training is available in NASAR wilderness medicine programs.

Evacuation Techniques

As the first aider, you must decide whether the injured party should be evacuated or not. This is sometimes not an easy decision, and you should only make it after considering all the alternatives. Some considerations are:

- What is the patient's problem (or problem list)?
- Considering the mechanism of injury, does any one of the medical problems need advanced levels of medical treatment?
- Will any of the patient's anticipated problems need advanced levels of medical treatment (for example, near-drowning victims who develop pulmonary edema)?

If the answer to either of the last questions is yes, we must evacuate, *unless* we are able to bring advanced treatment to the patient. If the injury is severe and the evacuation difficult, this may be the best alternative. The next questions is, how urgent is the need to evacuate? If the patient's condition cannot be stabilized and serious consequences will result from delay, speed must be the overriding consideration, which may justify speedy but more hazardous methods of evacuation like helicopters and rafts. Persons with some sort of advanced medical training are obviously in a better position to make these decisions.

If the victim needs advanced care but can be adequately stabilized (for example, he has a simple fracture), a slower, more controlled evacuation is in order. In some cases, especially if the injury is not severe, the patient is often embarrassed "to cause so much trouble" and will want to continue the trip. You may have to insist that his evacuation is for the good of the trip as well as his own health.

When planning the evacuation, confer with the first aid and evacuation teams to determine the best evacuation route. Some routes may be automatically ruled out once you have carefully considered the nature of the injury. If the injury is not disabling, the patient can often walk out on his own, and this is certainly easier than carrying him. But his condition could worsen, or he could become disoriented or lost. We have already seen that a patient may appear "shocky," and the rescuer needs to know whether it is real shock or ASR. As a precautionary measure, at least two people should be sent out with the patient, so that if his condition does worsen, one can stay with him and another can go for help. The first aider should stay with the patient all the way to the hospital. He is familiar with the injuries and vital signs and can monitor change more accurately. Perhaps more important, he and the patient will have developed a rapport that should not be interrupted.

In a very remote area, or if speed is essential and the surrounding terrain rough, or in a canyon, where overland evacuation is virtually impossible, the best means of evacuation may be the river (another alternative, helicopter evacuation, is discussed in chapter 7). Most patients with serious injuries are not anxious to get back on the water, and the flexing of an inflated boat can be painful even to the best-splinted fracture, but this may be the only alternative.

If you choose river evacuation, keep the following considerations in mind:

- Never tie a patient into a raft or onto a litter in a raft. In addition to the real danger of drowning if the raft flips, it is important to consider the patient's subjective feelings of fear.

- Two canoes can be lashed together, catamaran-style, for increased stability. The Telfer lower (see chapter 5) is an excellent method for transporting a patient across a river.

- You can line the easier rapids and carry the patient around the more difficult ones.

- If you must cross above dangerous rapids or falls, rig a belay line or a Telfer lower.

Lightly injured people can be carried for short distances with one- or two-man carries: the clothes drag (see figure 9.6) is for emergency use only; the fireman's carry (figure 9.7) or the cross-shoulder carry (figure 9.8) are often effective for transporting people from the water to shore; the piggyback (figure 9.9) is really only practical with light patients; the two-man carry (figure 9.10) requires a wide path. One of the most comfortable ways to carry someone is the rope coil, a technique borrowed from our climbing friends. You must have a rope long enough (60 feet or longer) to put into a climbing coil (see figures 9.11 and 9.12). The coiled rope then goes around the rescuer's shoulders so that the patient can sit in it.

Injuries of a more serious nature require a litter. Ready-made litters are ideal if available (some outfitters place them near potential trouble spots ahead of time). If they are not, you can construct them from all kinds of materials—all it takes is little imagination. Here are some examples:

Fig. 9.5. Deciding whether and how to evacuate a patient is not always easy.

Fig. 9.6. The clothes drag.

Fig. 9.7. The fireman's carry.

Fig. 9.8. The cross-shoulder carry.

Fig. 9.9. The two-handed carry (piggyback).

Fig. 9.10. The two-man carry.

- A rope litter can be improvised from two throw ropes. "Weave" it with a series of slip knots (see figure 9.13).

- Life jackets can be rigged on saplings or paddles.

- A canoe with the flotation removed can be used as a litter. A canoe slid crosswise along railroad tracks, using two rescuers as "dog teams," makes an excellent evacuation vehicle (see figure 9.14).

- A kayak or C-1 can also be used as a makeshift litter, as long as the walls and seat have been removed (see figure 9.15). This works best with higher-volume boats.

- Your imagination is the limit. River debris such as car hoods, lumber, and billboards have been used in emergencies.

Moving the Litter

Evacuations are hard work. The primary goals of the litter team are to keep the patient horizontal and to make the movement of the litter as smooth as possible.

Test any litter first with a healthy person. Designate one of the litter bearers as captain. This person will coordinate lifting, lowering, and movement. You should by now have selected and scouted the evacuation route, but it is still a good idea to have a scout in front of the litter team to pick the exact route around boulders, trees, and other obstacles.

More than six litter bearers will generally get in each other's way; other team members should stand by to relieve the bearers from time to time. The safest way to switch bearers is to put the litter down, but this takes time. A more expedient method is to switch one person at a time "on the fly." Relief bearers walk alongside and take over from the litter bearers when they start to tire. Only one bearer should switch at a time, and litter bearers should switch frequently, so that they don't get so tired they might drop the litter. Shoulder straps help distribute the load (see figure 9.17).

If the litter team is faced with an obstacle the bearers cannot step over, the bearers stay in one place and pass the litter to another team on the other side with a caterpillar pass.

In rugged terrain the patient must be tied into the litter. Foot straps, groin straps, and underarm restraint straps will keep him secure. Pad the straps and check the patient occasionally to see that everything is comfortable. If the patient is conscious, don't tie his arms: he can fend off branches, scratch itches, and generally not feel so helpless. Be sure, though, to tell the patient to hold on to the straps rather than to the side of the litter—remember the incident described at the beginning of this chapter.

Figs. 9.11–9.12. Two views of the rope-coil carry.

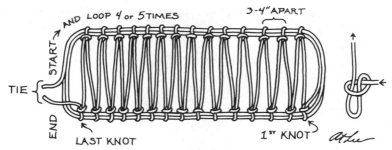

Fig. 9.13. Woven rope litter.

When moving a litter up a steep bank (something you often have to do in a river evacuation), a Talus belay is a useful technique (see figure 9.18). Tie two of your longest ropes to the head of the litter, then send a belayer as far as possible up the bank to select a belay point like a tree or boulder. The belayer should keep the rope taut as the litter is moved up the hill, so that if it falls the rope will keep it from bobsledding back down the bank. When the litter gets to the first belayer, a second belayer should repeat the process from the next belay point up the bank. In this way, the litter is always secured and you lose little time. This technique can also be used for moving a litter downhill.

Your responsibility to your patient doesn't automatically end when the evacuation team reaches an ambulance or rescue squad. In remote areas (particularly outside the United States) you may find volunteer rescue squads or ambulance personnel whose hearts are in the right place but who lack up-to-date training. Do they look organized, well supplied, and medically competent? Most squads and ambulance drivers should be EMTs (emergency medical technicians) and should be trained and equipped for patient care. If the medical authorities do not appear competent, you must continue the care of your patient until you find someone who can provide adequate care. This may require you to be direct and insistent about the manner of treatment, and it can be difficult if you are dealing with a legally constituted civil authority like a local search-and-rescue squad. If possible, the original first aider should accompany the patient to the hospital.

After any evacuation, take some time to discuss what happened. Mistakes can be identified while they're still fresh in everyone's mind. If the evacuation has been long and difficult and it's late, consider terminating the trip for the day.

Conclusion

Evacuations are no fun, but they are a very real part of whitewater rescue, and every paddler should have some basic knowledge of them. Professional outfitters and whitewater clubs often practice evacuations at potential trouble spots and have rescue gear (pulleys, backboards, first aid supplies) cached there. Quick, smooth evacuations save lives.

Fig. 9.14. A canoe can be used as an evacuation litter by towing it sideways along a railroad track. Many rivers have railroad tracks alongside them.

Fig. 9.15. Decked boats can also be used as improvised evacuation litters, although the walls and seat must usually be removed first. It's helpful to have someone stay with the boat to keep it from flipping over.

Fig. 9.16. An evacuation in progress. In extremely rough terrain like this, litter movement is a series of caterpillar passes. Good organization and route scouting are important. (Photo by Ellyn Feinroth/Nantahala Outdoor Center)

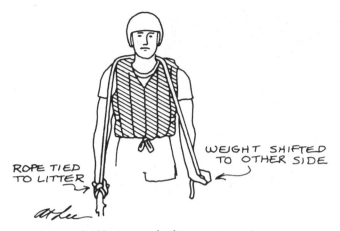

ROPE TIED
TO LITTER

WEIGHT SHIFTED
TO OTHER SIDE

Fig. 9.17. A shoulder strap makes litter carrying easier.

Fig. 9.18. The Talus belay alternatives belay points to provide security against the litter's slipping back down the bank. The litter should not be moved without one of the ropes on belay.

Training is everything. The peach was once a bitter almond; cauliflower is nothing but cabbage with a college education.

MARK TWAIN, *PUDD'NHEAD WILSON*

· 10 ·
The Professionals

So far, this book has been primarily directed toward the recreational whitewater user. We have described rescue systems based on equipment that a typical paddler might carry on a river trip, but we have not really discussed the specialized equipment and training that is the concern of the professional.

By "professional" we mean a person who makes his living on the river—that is, a guide, instructor, or boatman. These we will call river professionals. By guiding for hire, the whitewater professional assumes an added responsibility for the safety of his customers, who then are therefore entitled to rely on his expertise, training, and judgment. But there is another important type of professional: the search-and-rescue squad member, the firefighter, or the park ranger whose duty it is to rescue members of the public in trouble, and this large category of "rescue professionals" includes both amateurs and professionals, in the sense that some are paid to do their rescue work full-time and others, such as those belonging to volunteer fire departments and rescue squads, are unpaid part-timers. Representing a variety of agencies, these people try in general to prevent accidents and to save lives, but their level of training and expertise in whitewater rescue varies greatly.

In this chapter we will discuss some things both types of professional should consider about safety and rescue in their day-to-day operations. However, neither type exists in a vacuum, and each has areas of expertise and types of equipment that can benefit the other. Cooperation can be a problem: the rescue professional often ignores the wealth of experience of the river professional and regards him as an amateur, while the river professional too often regards the rescue professional as a threat to his operation. Especially on public lands, where the river companies are regulated by state or federal agencies, cooperation and understanding are essential, so we urge each type of professional to read the other's section of the chapter to get an idea of what is reasonable to expect.

Fig. 10.1. River and public service professionals can work together. Here a local rescue squad works with a river outfitter to develop swiftwater rescue skills.

The Rescue Professional

Professionals in almost any state may someday be faced with a whitewater rescue. Unfortunately, a significant percentage of the people who drown in the United States each year are rescue professionals who die in the line of duty. Preparation and training are vital.

Specialized training in river rescue is becoming available for the rescue professionals, but all would be well advised to study the earlier chapters of this book. There are many ways to do a whitewater or swiftwater rescue, and most of the techniques described in this book can easily be adapted to specific circumstances. At the very least, the rescue professional should be aware of the power of moving water and its hidden hazards and should know how to protect himself before trying to save others.

Preparation for the public service rescue professional means not only having the right equipment and knowledge of rescue techniques, but also studying the rivers in his agency's jurisdiction. As far as rescue is concerned, rivers fall into two broad categories: whitewater rivers that are regularly used for recreation, and other rivers and streams that are not normally swift but are subject to floods.

Many of the United States' whitewater rivers are in state and national parks; some are even in urban areas. These natural resources represent access to adventure for many outdoor enthusiasts. How public servants deal with these resources has a direct effect on the number of accidents that occur on them. Resource managers should know the safe capacities and limits of the rivers under their jurisdiction. They should know the access points, construct gauges to measure water levels, and establish "safe" levels for recreation. They may have to issue regulations concerning craft size and type and required safety gear, but this should be done sparingly. Information and warning signs can help the uninformed (see figure 10.2). Managers should identify hazards and disseminate information about them.

Fig. 10.2. River hazards, like highway hazards, can be marked on busy rivers.

In spite of these duties, managers should try to avoid undue restrictions on rivers during times of high water. Although it may be appropriate to set limits for commercial outfitters, setting them for a group of expert private boaters risking only themselves is not. Limiting expert private paddlers frequently creates a more dangerous situation than it eliminates, since the offending paddlers, who often sneak on anyway, are often prevented by the need for secrecy from making adequate safety plans.

The same thinking applies to equipment. Though there are some widely recognized standards, such as helmets for decked boaters and multiple air chambers for rafts, safety lies ultimately in the paddler's ability rather than in his equipment. The decision as to what rescue gear to carry should usually be left to the individual or group.

Where can resource managers learn about the river? personal involvement and research is the best way. A lot of answers (and questions) come from the users, both recreational paddlers and professional outfitters. Outfitters are usually more conservative in their outlook, because of liability considerations and the need to protect rental equipment. Some expert recreational paddlers, on the other hand, will tend to minimize difficulties and overestimate the skill level of the casual paddler.

But what about the rivers, streams, and creeks that aren't normally white-water but that become so in flood? Nearby inhabitants often have a wealth of information about these rivers: where they flood their banks, which low bridges go under first, how big the waves get at the narrows, and much more. Managers should look at the river at its normal level. Are there large piles of debris piled up in the trees or in certain bends or constrictions in the river? These could be strainers at higher water. Are the banks undercut? Are there manmade hazards such as low-head dams or fallen bridges? What is the gradient of that little stream, and what would it be like with ten times the flow? How big is the watershed, and what are the water-absorbing qualities of the soil? Runoff from areas upstream may cause radical and unpredictable rises after a rain. Keeping records or finding those that other agencies may be keeping will help managers to know many of these things, as will observing a river in all its moods throughout the year. In-depth knowledge will help prevent accidents.

In many areas, the river itself is the boundary of an agency's jurisdiction. This can cause problems if no one considers in advance *which* agency is

Fig. 10.3. Search-and-rescue organizations should be aware that not all hazards are obvious in times of low water. Low-water bridges, such as this one in West Texas, can form a deadly hydraulic during higher water.

responsible for the rescue. When an Air Florida jet crashed into the Potomac River in 1982 the result was a classic case of jurisdictional confusion. In some cases, especially in urban areas, it is better to have one unit trained and equipped for river rescue and to have all calls referred to that unit, regardless of jurisdictional boundaries.

There are many things government agencies can do to prevent river tragedies. The state of Ohio, for example, after several drownings among recreational paddlers and their would-be rescuers on rain-swollen rivers, initiated an aggressive policy of accident prevention. This has in some cases taken the form of warning signs near potential high-water trouble spots on normally calm rivers; in other cases, actual physical barriers have been erected to force paddlers to portage certain hazards like low-head dams. Manmade debris, bridge pilings (such as the one on the Ocoee mentioned in chapter 7), and defunct dams have been removed and some dams restructured to reduce the hydraulics at their base. Canoe liveries have been asked to place safety decals in their boats, and television programs have broadcast information on river levels and hazards. A number of these improvements have been paid for by river user fees.

A key aspect of successful river rescues is training. For most park rangers and firefighters, river rescue is a secondary aspect of the job. Because they do not normally work with whitewater they often lack an appreciation of its dangers and can unknowingly risk their lives in an emergency. Potential rescuers must know how to read water and spot potential capsize points, and they must be familiar with their equipment. However, the most important single aspect of any training program is probably teaching the rescuer to protect himself. He must know what constitutes a hazardous situation, how to avoid it, and, if avoidance fails, how to deal with it. There is no way to be comfortable around moving water without practice. Do it in a strictly controlled situation before it is really needed.

Having the right personal equipment (see chapter 2) is also important. A good life jacket and wetsuit should be considered mandatory for river rescuers: firefighters should *not* wear "turn out" coats and boots. Everyone should know the basics of swimming in whitewater, rope throwing, and mechanical rescues. Rescue courses such as the ones offered by the Nantahala Outdoor Center, Canyons, Inc., and others listed at the end of this book offer a safe and effective way for the rescue professional to learn from the river professionals.

Some Rescue Considerations for Professionals

We realize that not all public service professionals will be able to take river rescue courses, so we recommend the following sequence of operations to anyone who is faced with a whitewater or swiftwater rescue:

- Talk the victim into self-rescue if this is a safe option. Often a frightened or disoriented victim will overlook an obvious self-rescue alternative. At the very least, maintaining communication with the victim will help keep his hopes up while the rescue is being readied. Let him know what you intend to do and how.

- Use a shore-based rescue if possible. Do not jeopardize your safety or that of other rescuers unnecessarily. In addition to the techniques described in chapters 5, 6, and 7, a fire department team might use an extension ladder or fire hose rescue. In the latter, the fire house is inflated (see description below) to become a semirigid floating arm that can be extended to a victim stuck in low-head dam hydraulic or stranded on a rock.

- A boat-*assisted* rescue is more hazardous than one conducted from the shore but is safer than direction contact methods of rescue. The boat is used for ferrying tag lines, people, and equipment through calmer stretches of water above or below the rapid.

- A boat-*based* rescue requires contact with the victim. It's much more dangerous than the above systems because it exposes the rescuer to the same hazards as the victim. Consider the Telfer lower, tethered boat, or rope-assisted methods using tag lines and the like.

- A last-resort method is a contact rescue: a strong-swimmer or direct contact method. This poses great danger to the rescuer and should be considered last. The rescuer *must* be experienced in whitewater swimming and capable of self-rescue.

Professional Equipment

In addition to the equipment standard for any rescue organization, the following items can be very useful:

Line Guns. A line guns shoots a light haul line across the river (see figure 10.5). The rescuers then use the light line to haul over a heavier one, which eliminates the need for rope ferries. Rifle-type guns can shoot up to 800 feet, and crossbow versions will go about 200 feet. A bow and arrow with monofilament fishing line will work for narrow rivers.

Boogie Boards. California-based Rescue 3 uses these surfing craft extensively in its instruction program for ferries and even for "board-based" rescues (see figure 10.6). They are light and small enough to carry in an ambulance or in the trunk of a police car and can substitute for a boat in many situations. It is much easier to teach a novice to use a boogie board than to teach him to paddle a kayak or canoe.

Fig. 10.4. A rescue course at the Nantahala Outdoor Center.

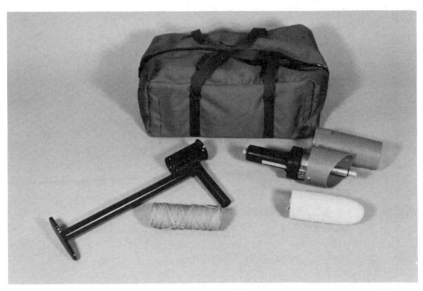

Fig. 10.5. The line gun provides a quick way of getting a rope across a river. (Photo courtesy Dive Rescue International)

Winches. A motor-driven or electrical winch light enough to be hand-carried to remote river sites can be very handy. Tackle blocks and steel cable, which does not stretch, will increase its capacity. If winches are not available, a simple "come-along" will suffice in most cases and is superior to a Z-drag.

Radios. Walkie-talkies and CB radios are very useful in almost any rescue situation, especially if they can communicate with rescue helicopters.

Helicopters. See chapter 7 for advantages and limitations.

Rope Bags. Long rope bags with 150–300 feet of half-inch kernmantle static rescue rope make management of rope for tag lines and rope ferries much easier.

Scoop Rigs, or "Billy Pugh Nets." This is a mesh scoop basket that can lift a victim from the water with a helicopter hoist (see figure 10.7). It is very useful on wide rivers.

Hose Rescue Device. This is an adapter for inflating fire hoses (see figure 10.8). Air-valve fittings are available for standard fire hoses (contact the Dayton, Ohio, Fire Department for details) which allow the hoses to be inflated to about 100 pounds per square inch. The rigid hose can then be extended for a shore-based rescue, providing a safe, inexpensive system for reaching a victim in the backwash of a low-head dam.

Boats. Most rescue organizations use hard boats (for example, a jon boat with an outboard motor), which are not really suited for whitewater use. Rafts (see below) are usually a better choice. Jet prop boats, on the other hand, can be used in moderate whitewater and on rivers so rocky they would ruin a normal propeller. A normal outboard can be converted to a jet prop, which propels the boat with a jet of water, with a kit. If you plan to use a prop boat, choose the propeller with power in mind rather than speed. All boats should be extremely careful in the backwash of low-head dams. The water in the backwash is very aerated, and neither normal nor jet props will work well in it. Several firefighters have drowned while attempting to motor up to victims held in a low-head dam hydraulic. One technique to use in this situation is to tether the boat nearest to the backwash to another boat downstream, well clear of the backwash. The downstream boat—whose propeller is in unaerated water—controls the progress of the first boat toward the dam. If the upstream boat gets caught in the backwash the downstream boat attempts to pull it out. If this fails the first boat can deliberately swamp and act as a "sea anchor" to pull the first one out.

Fig. 10.6. Originally designed for the surf, the boogie board has been adopted for river use by a number of professional organizations. It is easy to carry and requires less training than a kayak or canoe.

Inflatable Rafts. Rafts are much more stable and forgiving than boats and lend themselves to a variety of rescue techniques. Their separate air chambers make them virtually unsinkable. For rescue use a good size is 14–16 feet long and 6–8 feet wide. The raft should be able to carry six to eight people and can be propelled with paddles, oars, or an outboard motor. If your organization does not have its own, you might be able to borrow one from a nearby outfitter.

Catarafts. This may be the ideal river rescue craft. A cataraft consists of two inflatable pontoons joined together in a catamaran-type rig. The boat is very stable and can be propelled with oars or a motor. It can be instantly set up as a Telfer lower, cannot swamp, and, since there is very little current drag on the tubes, can enter the backwash of a low-head dam with far less chance of flipping or getting caught in the backwash than other craft.

The River Professional

The successful whitewater outfitter tries to run the "best" possible trip for his clientele. He wants his customers to enjoy the river experience, to be reasonably comfortable, and not to get hurt. He wants these people to return, and he knows that the words *safe* and *best* are in this respect interchangeable.

Responsible outfitters value their equipment and maintain it, knowing that they must periodically replace worn-out gear and rafts as they become unserviceable. They use the appropriate size of raft for the water they run and do not overload the boats so that they become difficult to control. Unfortunately, there are outfitters who do not do business this way. The popularity of whitewater rafting has attracted the inevitable marginal outfitters, who either cannot or will not put money into new equipment and guide training. Some, struggling to survive in a seasonal business, stretch the useful life of their equipment and employ poorly trained summer help.

Ideally, all guides should be thoroughly familiar with the river they will be working on, particularly if the trips are short, single-day trips. In multiday, expedition-style trips this is not always possible, but responsible outfitters will select staff who are experienced in reading water and who have proven boat-handling skills. These boatmen should have *current* CPR and first aid training. Trip leaders should have advanced first aid skills or be qualified EMTs. The outfitter's management should set standards and policies to ensure safe trips. Guidelines for safe water levels, weather conditions, and portages of dangerous rapids should be established in advance and not left solely to the discretion of the trip leader.

Other useful management policies address things like camp sanitation, speed limits and vehicle care, drug and alcohol abuse, and regulations on public land and rivers. Prudent outfitters will watch the policies of other companies carefully.

Fig. 10.7. The scoop net, shown here on a California Highway Patrol helicopter, can be lowered to victims with a helicopter-mounted winch. This is useful on rivers too wide to allow other systems to function effectively.

One area in which many outfitters are lax is that of rescue training—it doesn't earn them any money, and often they don't pay their employees for training time. But rescue skills are like any other skill: they atrophy with disuse. When the time comes, it is important that rescue knowledge be fresh in the rescuer's mind. Tyroleans, Telfers, and Z-drags are not the sort of thing you do every day; they should be relearned and practiced at least once a year, preferably before the high-water season.

Training like this is ideally done on the river on which you will work. Study rapids that have given trouble in the past and discuss which rescue system would work best. Each major rapid should have a general plan of rescue, including the evacuation route, worked out in advance. Often it is only by simulating the accident that you discover that you will need an extralong rope or other odd piece of gear. Some outfitters cache backboards, medical supplies, and other special gear at rapids that have a history of accidents.

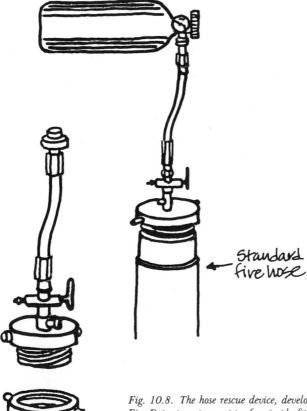

Standard fire hose

Fig. 10.8. The hose rescue device, developed by the Dayton, Ohio, Fire Department, consists of a simple fitting which allows rescuers to inflate a standard fire hose. The semi-rigid hose may then be extended to victims in places like low-head dam hydraulics.

Fig. 10.9. The cataraft may yet prove to be the ideal rescue craft. It is unswampable and lends itself to a variety of rescues. This one was prepared for the Durango Fire Department by Four Corners Marine and incorporates fore and aft rescue platforms.

Fig. 10.10. First aid training is an important part of working professionally on the river. Skills must be practiced to be effective.

A good training technique is the "accident scenario." The trainer should simulate an accident and give the trainees all the particulars: the nature of the injury, weather conditions, number of people available, and so on. The appointed rescue leader must effectively organize his people and care for the patient. He may also have to unpin a raft or boat and organize an evacuation. After the scenario is played out, the participants debrief as a group. The experience gained can be invaluable.

Conclusion

The skills the rescue professional needs are much the same as those the river professional needs. The rescue professional will have more and better equipment and support, but this is wholly or partly offset by the greater experience and knowledge of the river professional. All too often, pride is a factor on both sides: members of the search-and-rescue squad resent the amateurs in life jackets trying to tell them how to do their job; the whitewater outfitters are often reluctant to call for help because they prefer to handle their own problems. The only solution lies in increased awareness of the abilities and skills of each team. The search-and-rescue community must become more aware of the special problems and skills needed for whitewater and swiftwater rescue; river professionals must improve their own skills and actively work to promote good relationships with local public service professionals. Only in this way can all of us achieve our aim of safe, effective rescue.

Fig. 10.11. *Guides must know evacuation routes in advance. Walking the evacuation routes is part of the preseason training for these guides.*

Fig. 10.12. *A good way to practice rescue and evacuation skills is with an "accident scenario." These guides are practicing rescue from a pothole. This is the same pothole, at higher water, as the one shown in figure 1.3.*

Afterword

As interest in river recreation has grown, so has the number of unprepared paddlers. As a result, agencies responsible for public safety have been called upon to make swiftwater rescues with increasing frequency. Until fairly recently these operations were perilous at best. Basic techniques used by whitewater experts were not widely known in the search-and-rescue community. Few rescue units took any specialized training, and most of the rescues were improvised on the spot. The courage and ingenuity of these people notwithstanding, many of these attempts proved fatal to victims and rescuers alike.

Concerned with the backlash from these and other incidents and worried about restrictive legislation, professional river outfitters and whitewater clubs began working to spread knowledge of their skills to those who needed them. Assisted by boating-safety agencies in several states, a body of knowledge was developed specific to the needs of those in the field. We are now at the point where in some areas rescue professionals are capable of handling most situations and are constantly developing useful ideas based on their own operational needs. Sadly, this is not true in all areas of the country.

This book is for anyone who uses the river. If you have bought it to help you carry out your professional rescue responsibilities, it will not only give you a good background on the basics of river safety and rescue techniques, but also insight into the ways that rivers can be run responsibly. For more information on specific operational techniques suited to your needs, we suggest that you contact the sources of information and training listed at the back of the book under "Organizations" in the section "Further Sources of Information."

Charlie Walbridge
American Canoe Association safety chairman

Appendices

Appendix A
International Scale of
River Difficulty

This is the American version of a rating system used to compare river difficulty throughout the world. The system is not exact; rivers do not always fit easily into one category, and regional or individual interpretations may cause misunderstanding. It is no substitute for a guidebook or accurate first-hand descriptions of a run.

Paddlers attempting difficult runs in an unfamiliar area should act cautiously until they get a feel for the way the scale is interpreted locally. River difficulty may change each year due to fluctuations in water level, downed trees, geological disturbances, or bad weather. Stay alert for unexpected problems!

As river difficulty increases, the danger to swimming paddlers becomes more severe. As rapids become longer and more continuous, the challenge increases. There is a difference between running an occasional Class IV rapid and dealing with an entire river of this category. Allow an extra margin of safety between skills and river ratings when the water is cold if the river itself is remote and inaccessible.

The Six Difficulty Classes

Class I: Easy. Fast moving water with riffles and small waves. Few obstructions, all obvious and easily missed with little training. Risk to swimmers is slight; self-rescue is easy.

Class II: Novice. Straightforward rapids with wide, clear channels which are evident without scouting. Occasional maneuvering may be required; but rocks and medium-sized waves are easily missed by trained paddlers. Swimmers are seldom injured and group assistance, while helpful, is seldom needed.

Class III: Intermediate. Rapids with moderate, irregular waves which may be difficult to avoid and which can swamp an open canoe. Complex maneuvers in fast current and good boat control are often required; large waves or strainers may be present but are easily avoided. Strong eddies and powerful current effects can be found, particularly on large-volume rivers. Scouting is advisable for inexperienced parties. Injuries while swimming are rare; self-rescue is usually easy but group assistance may be required to avoid long swims.

Class IV: Advanced. Intense, powerful but predictable rapids requiring precise boat handling in turbulent water. Depending on the character of the river, it may feature large, unavoidable waves and holes or constricted passages demanding fast maneuvers under pressure. A fast, reliable eddy turn may be needed to initiate maneuvers, scout rapids, or

212 • River Rescue

rest. Rapids may require "must" moves above dangerous hazards. Scouting is necessary the first time down. Risk of injury to swimmers is moderate to high, and water conditions may make self-rescue difficult. Group assistance for rescue is often essential but requires practiced skills. A strong Eskimo roll is highly recommended.

Class V: Expert. Extremely long, obstructed, or very violent rapids which expose a paddler to above average endangerment. Drops may contain large, unavoidable waves and holes or steep, congested chutes with complex, demanding routes. Rapids may continue for long distances between pools, demanding a high level of fitness. What eddies exist may be small, turbulent, or difficult to reach. At the high end of the scale, several of these factors may be combined. Scouting is mandatory but often difficult even for experts. A very reliable Eskimo roll, proper equipment, extensive experience, and practiced rescue skills are essential for survival.

Class VI: Extreme. One grade more difficult than Class V. These runs often exemplify the extremes of difficulty, unpredictability, and danger. The consequences of errors are very severe and rescue may be impossible. For teams of experts only, at favorable water levels, after close personal inspection and taking all precautions. This class does *not* represent drops thought to be unrunnable, but may include rapids which are only occasionally run.

Appendix B
Universal River Signals

Stop: *Potential hazard ahead. Wait for "all clear" signal before proceeding, or scout ahead.* Form a horizontal bar with your outstretched arms. Those seeing the signal should pass it back to others in the party.

Help Emergency: *Assist the signaller as quickly as possible.* Give three long blasts on a police whistle while waving a paddle, helmet or life vest over your head. If a whistle is not available, use the visual signal along. A whistle is best carried on a lanyard attached to your life vest.

All Clear: *Come ahead. (In the absence of other directions proceed down the center.)* Form a vertical bar with your paddle or one arm held high above your head. Paddle blade should be turned flat for maximum visibility. To signal direction or a preferred course through a rapid around obstruction, lower the previously vertical "all clear" by 45 degrees toward the side of the river with the preferred route. Never point toward the obstacle you wish to avoid.

Appendix C
The Force of Water

The force of water against an obstacle does not, as you might expect, increase in linear proportion to the velocity of the current. If a current of 3 feet per second exerts a force of 17 foot-pounds on your legs, you might reasonably think that a 6-feet-per-second current would exert a force of 34 foot-pounds. *This is not so.* The force of water increases in proportion to the *square* of the velocity of the current. Thus, if the current velocity doubles, the force of the water increases fourfold.

Current Velocity	Average Total Force of Water (foot-pounds)		
(feet per second)	*(on legs)*	*(on body)*	*(on swamped boat)*
3	16.8	33.6	168
6	67.2	134.0	672
9	151.0	302.0	1512
12	269.0	538.0	2688

Appendix D
Useful Knots

Double Fisherman's Knot: Also used to tie together two pieces of rope, this knot is good when the ropes are substantially different in diameter, but it is very difficult to untie after being put under tension.

Simple Prusik: Named for its inventor, Dr. Karl Prusik, this knot has many uses in river rescue. Its main virtue is that it will grip when under tension but stay loose when not.

Simple Bowline with Stopper: Easy to tie, this knot must be tied off or backed up in some way so that it will not loosen when not under tension. Feeding the free end back through the eye of the knot works well as a safety. This knot is not difficult to untie after use.

Figure-of-Eight Family of Knots: The Figure Eight knot is strong, simple to remember, and easy to untie and to verify visually that it is tied correctly. The four variations shown below will serve almost any purpose on the river.

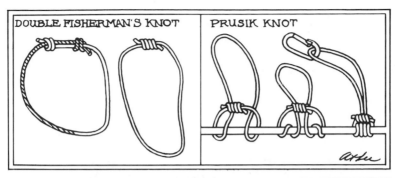

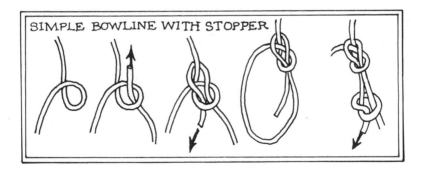

Figure Eight Follow Through: a strong knot to tie two lines together. Use this rather than the Double Fisherman's if you want to untie the lines later. Both this and the next knot are sometimes called "tracer" knots.

Figure Eight Follow Through Loop: Climbers use this knot for tying into a sit harness, and it can be used for any situation that requires a loop around something.

thing. It is less likely to untie when not under tension than a bowline.

Figure Eight on a Bight: A quick, easy, and strong way to put a loop at the end of a rope, or anywhere along it.

Double-Loop Figure Eight: Use this when you want to double a line for increased strength, such as for a doubled haul line, or for two anchor points.

FIGURE OF EIGHT FAMILY OF KNOTS

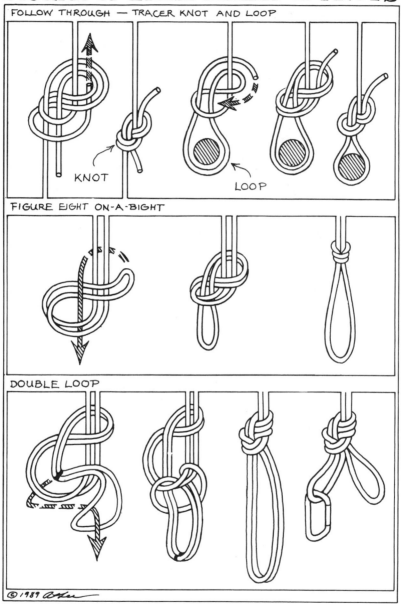

FOLLOW THROUGH — TRACER KNOT AND LOOP

KNOT

LOOP

FIGURE EIGHT ON-A-BIGHT

DOUBLE LOOP

© 1989

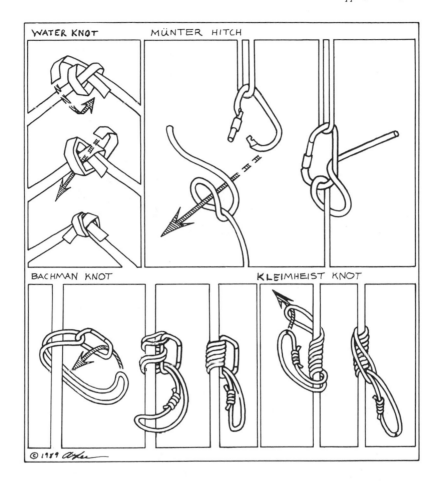

Water Knot: A simple overhand knot to join pieces of webbing.

Münter Hitch: A simple and effective belay system which uses the friction of the rope against itself, the Münter works best on a large carabiner with a smooth radius such as the Chouinard "Peara-biner." The hitch will work in either direction and requires only a carabiner to function.

Bachmann Knot: A cinching knot similar to the prusik except that it works only in one direction, the Bachmann uses a prusik loop wrapped around a carabiner, which provides a convenient handle. The Bachmann knot's best application is as a substitute for a brake prusik. The carabiner will not pass through the anchor pulley/carabiner of a Z-drag and so does not need to be monitored.

Kleimheist Knot: This is another cinching knot that can be used in place of a prusik if you are using webbing rather than cord. Like the Bachmann, it works in only one direction.

Appendix E
Cold Water Survival Chart

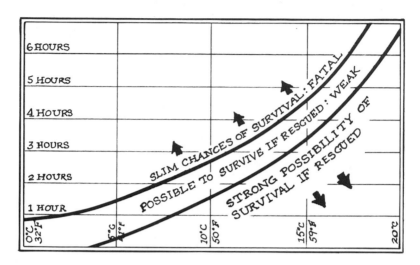

Appendix F
First Aid Kit

1. "Ouch Pouch" for Day Trips

Ten 1" adhesive bandages
24" of half-inch adhesive tape
8 gauze pads (four 4" x 4", four 2" x 2")
Roll of gauze (2" wide)
10 aspirin or aspirin substitute
Sunscreen
Lip balm
Butane lighter
Pocket mask
Sterile gloves
Anaphylaxis kit (injectable epinephrine)
Trauma scissors
Povidone-iodine ointment or solution
Triangular cravat (1)

2. Group Kit for Day Trips, Divided into Three Parts

Quick-access bag
20 aspirin or aspirin substitute
Ten 1" adhesive bandages
Roll of adhesive tape
4 large safety pins
Sunscreen
Povidone-iodine ointment or solution
Anaphylaxis kit (injectable epinephrine)
Glucose (oral)
Sterile gloves (2 pair)
Pocket mask
Trauma scissors

Trauma bag
Ten 1" adhesive bandages

20 gauze pads (ten 4" x 4", ten 2" x 2")
2 rolls of gauze strip (2" wide)
Trauma dressing (gauze)
2 triangular cravats
2 tampons
4 elastic roller bandages (2")
Roll of adhesive tape
Chemical cold pack
Bottle of eyewash solution
Hand towel
Combine dressing (2)

Materials bag
Tweezers
Snake-bite kit (suction)
2 finger splints
Butane lighter
Small flashlight
Emergency "space blanket"
3 ammonia inhalants
Nylon stretcher
First aid book
Leg splint
Full arm splint
Hypothermia thermometer
Lubricating jelly (small tube)
Blanket pins (2)
Syringe (60 cc)

Tongue depressors (2)
Oral airway (3 sizes)
N-P airway
Heat packs (optional for cold weather)

3. *Expedition Recommendations*

This kit would include all the contents of the group kit for day use, with the number of individual items increased according to the length of the expedition and the number of participants. The additional items below require training in their use and should be varied according to the medical background of the members of the expedition.

Blood pressure cuff
Stethoscope
Thermometers (oral and hypothermia)
Adult airway
Bulb syringe (for suction)
Intravenous kit
Drug kit
Tooth-fracture kit

Appendix G
Ground-to-Air
Signals for Survivors

These signals are intended for communication with a helicopter. They are advisory, and a pilot is under to obligation to obey them. When these signals are used, it is important that the signaler be positioned beyond the path of the main rotor where he may be readily seen.

Clear to start engine. Make a circular motion above your head with your right arm.

Hold on ground. Extend your arms horizontally, thumbs pointing down.

Move the helicopter forward. Extend your arms forward and wave the helicopter toward you.

Clear to lift. Extend your arms horizontally, palms up.

Move to signaler's right. Extend your right arm horizontally and motion to your right with the palm of your left hand.

Move the helicopter back. Extend your arms forward and "push" the helicopter away.

Move to signaler's left. Extend your left arm horizontally and motion to your left with the palm of your right hand.

Release sling load. Touch your left forearm with your right hand, palm extended.

Land here: My back is into the wind. Extend your arms toward the landing area with the wind at your back.

Cleared for takeoff. Extend both arms above your head, thumbs up.

Shut down. Cross your neck with your right hand, palm down.

Wave off: Do not land. Wave your arms from the side to over your head.

The following signals are generally used for attracting the attention of the pilots of fixed-wing aircraft, though they may also attract a helicopter. Make the signs by placing rocks on the ground, spreading out clothing, scratching in the dirt, or stamping in the snow. In any case, make the signs large enough to be visible from high above.

V   *Require assistance*

X   *Require medical assistance*

N   *No (or negative)*

Y   *Yes (or affirmative)*

↑   *Proceeding in this direction*

Signals for pilots

Indicate wind direction. Circle.

No. Yaw back and forth.

Yes. Pitch up and down.

Appendix H
Cardiopulmonary
Resuscitation (CPR)

When a person's heart and lungs stop functioning because of shock, drowning, a heart attack, or other causes, it is possible to save that life by administering cardiopulmonary resuscitation, or CPR.

CPR provides artificial circulation and breathing for the victim. External cardiac compressions administered manually are alternated with mouth-to-mouth resuscitation in order to stimulate the natural functions of the heart and lungs.

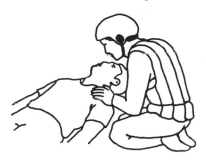

1. ***Determine whether the victim is unconscious.*** Tap or gently shake the victim's shoulder. Shout "Are you OK?" If there is no response, shout "Help!" (Someone nearby may be able to assist.) Do the Airway step next.

2. ***Airway step.*** Place one hand on the victim's forehead and push firmly back. Hook the fingers of the other hand on the bony part of the lower jaw and lift up and forward on the chin until the teeth are almost closed. Tip the head until the chin points straight up. This should open the airway. Place your ear near the victim's mouth and nose. LOOK at the chest for breathing movements, LISTEN for breaths, and FEEL for breathing against your cheek. If there is no breathing, do the Quick step next.

3. ***Quick step.*** Give two slow, independent breaths. To do this, keep the victim's head tipped and pinch his nose. Open your mouth wide and take a deep breath. Make a good seal on the victim's mouth, then give the breaths, watching for the chest to rise.

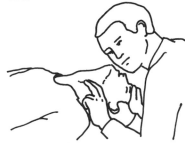

4. ***Check step.*** CHECK the pulse and breathing for at least five but no more than ten seconds. To do this,

keep the victim's head tipped with your hand on his forehead. Place the fingertips of your other hand on his Adam's apple and slide your fingers into the groove at the side of the neck nearest you. If there is a pulse but no breathing, give one breath every five seconds. If there is no pulse *or* breathing, send someone for emergency assistance while you locate the proper hand position for chest compression. Begin chest compressions.

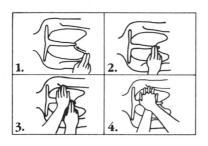

5. ***Hand position for chest compressions.*** (A) With your middle and index fingers find the lower edge of the victim's rib cage on the side nearest you. (B) Trace the edge of the ribs up to the notch where the ribs meet the breastbone. (C) Place your middle finger *on* the notch, your index finger next to it. Put the heel of your other hand on the breastbone next to the fingers. (D) Put your first hand on top of the hand on the breastbone. Keep the fingers off the chest.

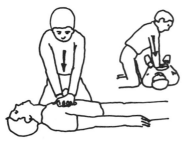

6. ***Chest compressions.*** *Push straight down,* without bending your elbows, always maintaining the proper hand

position. Keep your knees a shoulder width apart. Your shoulders should be directly over the victim's breastbone. Keep your hands along the midline of his body. Bend from your hips, not your knees. Keep your fingers off the victim's chest. Push down 1½ to 2 inches. Count "1 and, 2 and, 3 and . . . " and so on.

7. ***Push 15—Breathe 2.*** Give 15 compressions at a rate of 80–180 per minute. Tip the victim's head so the chin points up and give two quick full breaths. Continue to repeat 15 compressions followed by two breaths. Check the pulse and breathing after the first minute and every few minutes thereafter. NOTE: *Do not practice chest compressions on people—you might cause internal injuries.*

This information does not take the place of CPR training. Contact your local Red Cross or American Heart Association chapter to find out how you can learn this life-saving procedure.

Appendix I
Symptoms of Hypothermia

Body Temperature: The hypothermia victim has a core (internal body) temperature that is lower than normal. The following list shows the successive stages of the condition:

Moderate

Above 95°F. The victim is conscious and alert and may have vigorous shivering.

90°–95°F. The victim is conscious but has mild to moderate clouding of mental faculties. Shivering is present but diminished.

Severe

86°–90°F. The victim has severe clouding or consciousness, may even be unconscious. Shivering is replaced by muscular rigidity.

Below 86°F. The victim is unconscious, with diminishing respirations.

Below 80°F. The victim has barely detectable or nondetectable respirations.

Blood Pressure and Pulse: Blood pressure is lower than normal (frequently less than 100 mm mercury systolic). Pulse is generally slow and often irregular; it may be difficult to find it at all in the extremities because of blood vessel constriction—measure the heart rate in the neck at the carotid artery or in the groin at the femoral artery.

General Appearance: The victim is pale in appearance and his skin is very cold to the touch. In fact, his skin and subcutaneous tissues are often at the temperature of the water he was immersed in. The victim's pupils begin to dilate at temperatures around 92°F and are fully dilated and poorly reactive to light at around 86°F.

Appendix J
Patient Assessment System (PAS)

I. **Survey Scene**
Danger
Mechanism

II. **Primary Survey**
A—Airway
B—Breathing
C—-Circulation
D—Disability

III. **Secondary Survey**
Head
Eyes
Ears
Nose
Mouth/Throat
Neck
Chest
Abdomen
Pelvis
Genitalia
Legs
Arms
Back
Buttocks
Neuro

IV. **Vital Signs**
T—Time
BP—Blood Pressure
P—Pulse
R—Respiration
C/MS—Consciousness/Mental Status
T—Temperature
S—Skin Color

V. **History**
A—Allergies
M—Medications
P—Past History
L—Last Meal
E—Events

VI. **SOAP**
S—Subjective
O—Objective
A—Assessment
P—Plan for Treatment

VII. **Monitor**
S
O
A/A = Problems/Anticipated Problems
P

PAS Notes

I. Survey Scene

1. **Danger**—Immediate danger to victim or rescuer (falling rock, explosions, etc.).

2. **Mechanism**—Trauma vs. illness (fall, sudden chest pain, MVA, etc.). Both may be possible. Determine possible mechanism for spine injury.

This survey is done before or during approach to the victim. It is done quickly and generally takes no extra time.

II. Primary Survey

	Green Flags	*Red Flags*
A—Airway	air in/out	no air in/out
B—Breathing	ventilation adequate	ventilation not adequate
C—Circulation	1. pulse 2. no severe bleeding	1. no pulse 2. severe bleeding
D—Disability	1. no mechanism for spine injury 2. consciousness *A*VPU	1. mechanism for spine injury 2. consciousness A*V*PU

1. Primary Survey can be performed with all elements done in sequence or done simultaneously. Stop and treat problems (Red Flags) as they are found. Survey and treatment of problems may be done simultaneously.

2. Basic Life Support (BLS) is treatment of problems in the Primary Survey. Cardiopulmonary Resuscitation (CPR) is a limited form of BLS that is more useful for illness than for trauma.

3. The term *Primary Assessment* is sometimes used for: I. Survey Scene + II. Primary Survey.

Reproduced courtesy of the National Association for Search and Rescue.

Other Sources of
Information

Books

River Rescue

Ohio Department of Natural Resources, Division of Watercraft. *River Rescue*. Columbus: Ohio State University, 1980.
Training manual for emergency services personnel, with emphasis on low-head dam rescue. Ohio DNR is a pioneer agency in swiftwater rescue.

Medical

Emergency Care and Transportation of the Sick and Injured, 4th ed. Chicago: The American Academy of Orthopaedic Surgeons, 1987.
EMT textbook, with all the gruesome details. Mainly geared to short-term ambulance care.

American Heart Association. *Cardiopulmonary Resuscitation*. Tulsa: CPR Publishers, 1986.
The latest reference on CPR from the American Heart Association, covering recent changes in CPR procedures.

American Red Cross. *(Standard and) Advanced First Aid & Emergency Care,* and *Cardiopulmonary Resuscitation.* Garden City, N.Y.: Doubleday, 1979.
Red Cross textbooks. The minimum standard for any whitewater paddler. Take the courses!

Wilkerson, James A., ed. *Hypothermia, Frostbite, and Other Cold Injuries.* Seattle: The Mountaineers, 1986.
The best book currently available on the subject(s). Good section on water-related cold injuries and drowning complications.

Wilkerson, James A., ed. *Medicine for Mountaineering,* 2nd ed. Seattle: The Mountaineers, 1975.
The bible for wilderness medical emergencies. In-depth treatment of medical problems beyond first aid.

Paddling and Rafting

McGinnis, William. *The Guide's Guide: Reflections on Guiding Professional River Trips.* El Sobrante, Calif.: Whitewater Voyages, 1981.
This is the book Whitewater Voyages uses to instruct its own guides. A compendium of solid, practical, whitewater information.

McGinnis, William. *Whitewater Rafting.* New York: Quadrangle/The New York Times Book Company, 1975.
Bill McGinnis pioneered many of the difficult (Class V) rivers in California. His experience and philosophy of running trips makes worthwhile reading.

Nealey, William. *Kayak*. Birmingham, Ala.: Menasha Ridge Press, 1986.
An entertaining cartoon book about advanced kayak technique, this book is not just for fun. The sections on rescue are excellent and current, as are the sections on water reading and hydraulic phenomena. Highly recommended for any paddler contemplating Class III and above water.

Rowe, Ray. *White Water Kayaking*. London: Salamander Books, 1988.
Probably the best general guide to kayaking in English, this little book manages to cover everything from Eskimo rolling to rescue. Well worth reading. Rowe organized the 1988 International Safety Symposium in Nottingham, U.K.

Watters, Ron. *The White-Water River Book*. Seattle: Pacific Search Press, 1982.
Excellent general guide to paddling organization, equipment, water reading, and safety. Recommended.

Safety

Walbridge, Charlie, ed. *Best of the River Safety Task Force Newsletter 1976–1982*. Lorton, Va.: American Canoe Association, 1983.
The best of the worst.

Walbridge, Charlie, ed. *River Safety Report 1982–1985*. Lorton, Va.: American Canoe Association, 1986.
Compilation of river accidents and the source of much of the information in this book. This—and the companion volume above—are must reading for any paddler.

Technical Ropes and Mountaineering

Frank, James A., and Jerrold B. Smith. *Rope Rescue Manual*. Santa Barbara, Ca-

lif.: California Mountain Company, 1987.
In-house book by a company specializing in rope rescue. Excellent in-depth treatment of knots, ropes, hardware, and raising and lowering systems.

May, W. G. *Mountain Search and Rescue Techniques*. Boulder, Colo.: Rocky Mountain Rescue Group, 1973.
Good, if somewhat dry, technical mountaineering text, with info on ropes, brakes, haul systems, and so on.

Padgett, Allen, and Bruce Smith. *On Rope*. Huntsville, Ala.: National Speleological Society, 1987.
If you're a dedicated rope jock, this is the book to have. Exhaustive treatment of everything rope related. Recommended.

Setnicka, Tim. *Wilderness Search and Rescue*. Boston: Appalachian Mountain Club, 1980.
A standard reference work on the technical aspects of rescue: ropes, knots, pulleys, friction, Tyroleans, and so forth. Written mainly for climbers, the whitewater section is dated. Recommended for those interested in technical aspects of ropework. The helicopter section is also excellent.

Helicopters

Helicopter Operations and Personnel Safety (Helirescue Manual). Survival Education Association, 9035 Golden Givens Road, Tacoma, WA 98845, 1972.
Excellent technical reference on working with helicopters.

Foreign

Kanu-Gefahren. Munich, West Germany: Alpiner Kajak-Club, 1983.
If you're looking for the edge, this is it.

A slim volume with some hair-raising photos and Germanic ideas of kanuing rescue. In German.

Machatshek, Holger. *Richtig Wildwasserfahren.* Munich, West Germany: BLV Verlagsgesellschaft, 1986.
An excellent text (if you read German) on the state of river running in Central Europe. Good sections on harnesses and other technical river rescue gear.

Reithmaier, Peter. *Sicherheit in Wildwasser.* Mils, Austria: Private edition, 1985.
Austrian safety text. The author manufactures rescue gear and hosted the 1985 Canoesport Safety Symposium in Mayerhofen, Austria. In German.

Magazine Articles

Kaiser, Dr. Kenneth. *"Whitewater Medicine,"* Wilderness Medicine, July 1987.
An excellent discussion of field methods for reducing shoulder dislocations, as well as several other medical considerations for the paddler.

Videos

Margin for Error
The Uncalculated Risk
Whitewater Primer

American Red Cross
17th and D St.
Washington, DC 20006

River Rescue, by Anne Ford and Les Bechdel

Gravity Sports
100 Broadway
Jersey City, NJ 07306
800-346-4884

Whitewater Boating: A Safe Beginning

KUSA-TV
1089 Bannock St.
Denver, CO 80204

Whitewater Boating is also available through the National Organization for River Sports.

The Drowning Machine

Film Space
615 Clay St.
State College, PA 16801

Organizations

Alpiner Kajak-Club
Stundzstrasse 21
D-8000 München 80
West Germany

Europe's premier paddling club. AKC paddlers pioneered many of Europe's most difficult runs.

American Canoe Association
Box 248
Lorton, VA 22079

The largest paddling organization in the U.S., covering flatwater, whitewater, and racing.

American Whitewater Affiliation
146 Brockway
Palatine, IL 60067

A whitewater paddling organization with a strong emphasis on river conservation.

Canyons Incorporated
Box 823
McCall, ID 83638
208-634-4303

In addition to Idaho wilderness trips, Canyons president and *River Rescue* co-author Les Bechdel probably teaches more rescue courses than anybody. Your place or his.

> Canyonlands Field Institute
> Box 68
> Moab, UT 84532
> 801-259-7750

Specializing in big water rescue for western river outfitters.

> Nantahala Outdoor Center
> US 19W, Box 41
> Bryson City, NC 28713
> 704-488-2175

Whitewater professionals. Courses in river rescue for the recreational paddler and the search-and-rescue professional who must do onsite rescues.

> National Association for Search and
>   Rescue
> P.O. Box 3709
> Fairfax, VA 22038
> 207-665-2707

The NASAR Wilderness Medicine Programs—Wilderness EMT (EMT-W) and Wilderness First Responder, and Wilderness First Aid—are among the best available. They produce trained, certified professionals.

> National Organization for River
>   Sports
> Box 6847
> Colorado Springs, CO 80904

A Colorado-based organization composed primarily of western private paddlers.

> Ohio Department of Natural
>   Resources
> Division of Watercraft
> Fountain Square
> Columbus, OH 43224

Pioneers in swiftwater rescue training, with emphasis on dealing with low-head dams. Manuals and courses available.

> Rescue 3
> Box 1686
> Sonora, CA 95370

Professional training organization giving courses primarily on the West Coast.

> Rigging for Rescue (the technical
>   ropework school)
> Box 399
> Invermere, British Columbia
> VOA 1KO
> 604-342-6042

Arnor Larson's technical rope school is well respected in the climbing and rescue communities.

Index

NOTE: Numbers in **boldface** indicate pages on which illustrations or major discussion of the entry are found.

Accident prevention, 1, 15–16, 21, 50–51, 199
"Accident scenario," 208, **209**
Airbags, 44, 48–49
Aircraft, signals for, **222**
American Canoe Association (ACA), 22
  River Safety Task Force, 53, 57
  Safety Committee, 174
American River, **14**
American Whitewater Affiliation (AWA)
  International Scale of River Difficulty, 12–13, **211–212**
Anchor line, 32–38
  passing a knot on, 148, **149**
  for Telfer lower, 100, **101–103, 105, 106**
  for Tyrolean rescue, 147–148, 151
Anchor point, 100, 129–130, 133, **137**
  for Tyrolean rescues, 146, 147–148
Arkansas River, 3
"Armstrong" method of boat recovery, 118, **119**
Autonomic stress syndrome (ASR), 177–178

Base camp, 169, 170
Bear hug rescue, **179**
Bechdel, Les, 33, 134, 174–175
Belaying techniques
  body, **64, 68**
  dynamic, **68–70**, 75
  friction, **69**
  Münter hitch, 31, 105, **106, 148**
  static, **68**, 75
  Talus belay, 192, **194**
  in Telfer lower, 100–106
Bernard, Rick, 116
Berry, Karen, 159–161

Best of the River Safety Task Force Newsletter, 22, 57, 155, 156
"Billy Pugh Nets." *See* Scoop rigs
Bío-Bío River, 174–175
Blackadar, Walt
  "Blackadar handle," 46
Boat-based rescue, 87–88, 168, 200
  equipment retrieval, 94–99
  Eskimo rescue, 87, **88**
  of swimmers, **88–94**
  Telfer lower, 92, 98, 100–106
Boat pins, **108–111**
  extrication, 82, 118
  prevention, 46, 48
  recovery, 118–138
  rescue techniques, 76–81, 114–118
Boat recovery, 46, **97–98**
  See also Boat pins
Boats, chase, 87, 88, 168
Boats, decked, **42–46**
  as litters, **193**
  recovery of, 97–99
  rescue techniques, 87–88
  rescuing swimmers from, 90, **91–92**
  self-rescue, **52–53**, 54, **61–62**
  See also C-1s; Kayaks; Tethered boat rescue
Boats, rescue, 202
Boats, submerged, rescuing, 81, **98**, 118–119
Body rappel, 140
Boil line, **7, 11, 63**
Boogie boards, 200, **203**
Boulder sieves, **2**, 3, 10
Bridge lowers, 115, 139, 140, **159–161**
  rigging for, 140, **141–145**, 147, 148
Broaching, 60–61, **109**
Broach loop, **45**, 46, 114, 115

Broach rescue, 114
"Buddy boats," 16, 18
"Bulldozer" method of boat recovery, 46, 97, **98**
Bull Sluice, **4, 5**
Butterfly knot, **117**

C-1s, 94, 110, 114
  as litters, 190, **193**
Canoes, open, **48–49**
  entrapment in, 110–111
  as litters, 190, **193**
  recovery techniques, 97, **119–122, 123**
  rescue with, 92, 100, **101**
  self-rescue, 54, 55, **56, 59,** 62
Capistrano flip, 55, **56**
Carabiners, **26,** 27, **28, 29–31,** 145
  carabiner brake system, 143
  carabiner chains, 100, 104, **105, 153**
  Chouinard, **30,** 31
  Pearabiner, **30, 34**
  as pulleys, **128–129**
Cardiopulmonary resuscitation. *See* CPR
Cataraft (spider boat), 42, 100, 204, **207**
Caterpillar pass, 190
Chattooga River, 3
  hazards, 3, **5, 6, 9,** 57
  rescue on, 176
Cheat River, 156
Chest harness, 27, 144, **146**
  quick-release, 40
  See also Rescue harness
Clearwater River, 22
Cleat, jam, 46, **47, 48**
Clothes drag, 186, **188**
Clothing, **35–38**
Cockpits
  breakaway, 44, 45, 63
  keyhole, 44, **45**
Cold water survival chart, **218**
Colorado River, 3, **10, 51**
Communication team, 169–170
Contact rescue, 108, 113–115, 168, 200
CPR, 113, **179–181,** 204, **223–224, 227**
Cradle rig, 119, **122**
Cross-chest carry, **179**
Cross-shoulder carry, 186, **189**
Current strength, 123–124, **125, 138, 214**

Dams, low-head, **7, 11, 12,** 198, 199
  rescue boats for, 202
  rescue techniques, **63,** 77, **78,** 94, 139
Dayton, Ohio, Fire Department, 202, 206
Death
  liability for, 171
  reactions to, **173,** 174–175
  what to do in event of, 172–174
Debris, 10, 63, 190, 198, 199
"Deseret" scale for grading rapids, 13
D-rings, 31, 41, 100, 124, **143**
Drowning, 22, 53, 174–175
  "flush drowning," 12
  and hypothermia, 182
  life-saving techniques, **179–181**
Drysuits, 35, 36
Dülfer wrap, 140, **142**

Eddy, **2,** 4
  eddy turn, 57, **58**
  maneuvering swimmer into, **66,** 67, 82, **83**
Elevation loss, 3
Ellaho River, 10
Emergency kit, **24,** 35
EMTs (Emergency Medical Technicians), 177, 192, 204
Entrapment, **7, 9,** 43, 45, **108–109,** 110
  rescue techniques, 60–61, 63, 79–81, **113–118**
  steps in rescue, 111–113
  See also Foot entrapment
Equipment, 23
  maintaining, 50–51, 204
  preparing, 14
  professional rescue, 199, 200–204
  repair, 14
  retrieval, 94–98, **99**
  safety equipment, 23, **24–35,** 45–49
  See also Kayak Rescue Kits
Eskimo rescue, 87, **88**
Eskimo rolls, **52,** 53
Evacuation
  of entrapment victims, 113
  helicopter, 156–158, 162
  routes, 190, 206, **209**
  team, 169
  techniques, 185–194
Extrication
  of entrapped victims, 112–118

extrication team, 169
haul systems, 124–135
of pinned boats, 82, 118

Ferries, 57, **58,** 100, 107
rope, **76–77**
tension, **85–86**
Fiberglass boats, 44
Fire hoses, 202, **206**
Fireman's carry, 186, **188**
First Aid
kit, 18, **34–35, 218–219**
need for training, 176–177, 204, 206,
207
team, 169
treatment for shoulder dislocation,
185
See also CPR
Fixed-line rescue, 84, **85**
Flip lines, 42, **54**
Floating tag line, **77–79,** 111–112, 118
Flotation foam, 39
blocks, **48–49**
walls, 43, **44**
Flotation ring, 79
Foot braces, 43, **44**
Foot entrapment, 57, 59, 60, **80–81,**
84, 85, 112
Four Corners Marine, 207

Gauley River, 3, 115
Girth hitches, **28**
Grab loops, 46, 114, 119
"Grand Canyon" system of rating
rapids, 13

Haul lines, 38
Haul systems, **124–137**
Helicopters, 113, 139, 152
evacuation by, 156–158, 162
ground-to-air signals, **219–221**
rescue by, 154–156, 202
scoop rigs, 202, **205**
Helmets, 23, **29,** 50
Holes, **2, 4–7**
rescue from, **89**
self-rescue, **61–63**
Horizon line, **18**
Hose rescue device, 202, **206**
Hydraulics, **2,** 6, **7,** 10, 11, **12**
ledge hydraulic, **2**

rescue techniques for, **62–63,** 77–79,
88–89
Hypothermia, 12, 35, 54, 179, **182–183**
immersion, 182
rewarming techniques, 182, 183
symptoms, 225
wind-chill, 182

Injuries, 117, 124, 176, 177, 184–185

Jet props, 202

Karls, Bob, 155–156
Kayaks
entrapment in, 45, 109–110
equipment for, **24**
hazards of, 45, 46
with keyhole cockpit, **44, 45**
as litter, 190, **193**
paddle retrieval, 94, 97
Rescue Kit, **34**
rescues with, **91**
Safety Deck, 44, **45**
self-rescue, 62, 63
See also Boats, decked; Squirt boats
Kern River, 154
Knives, **33–34**
Knots, 31–32, **214–217**
Bachmann, 130, 133, **217**
bowline, 214, **215**
butterfly, **117**
double figure of eight, 148, 151, **154,**
214, **215, 216**
double fisherman's knot, 148, 214,
215
Kleimheist, 32, 130, **217**
passing, 148, **149**
tracer knots, 215, **216**
water knots, **217**
See also Loop knots; Prusiks

Landing zone, helicopter, 156–157, **158**
Leader, trip, 16, 18, 19, **20–21**
Leadership in rescue process, **20,** 163,
166, 168–169
Liability, 171, 197–198
Life jackets, 23, **24–27,** 50–51, 199
as litters, 190
modifying, **26–27**
Type III, 24–25
Type V, 25
Lifelines, 38

Line gun, 200, **201**
Litters, 186, 190
  moving, 190, 192–194
  switching bearers, 190, **193**
Loop knots, 31–32

Mammalian Diving Reflex (MDR), 181
Media, 171–172
Mid-current lowers, 83, **84**
Münter hitch, 30, 144, 145, **217**
  belaying with, 31, 103, 105, **106, 148**

Nantahala Falls, 13
Nantahala Outdoor Center (NOC), **201**
NASAR (National Assoc. for Search
  and Rescue), 177, 178, 227
Nenana River, **138**
NOC knot trick, **117**
Norton, John, 159–161

Ocoee River, 134
  Powerhouse Rapid rescue, **141**, 142,
  159–161
Oetz River, **12**
Ohio, state of
  accident prevention, 199
  Dept. of Natural Resources, 79
Organization, trip, **16–18**
Organization for rescue, 163–166
  priorities, 167
  rescue system selection, 167–168
  teams, 170
Outboard boats, 202
Outfitting
  decked boats, 42–47
  open canoes, 48–50
  rafts, 42
    double and triple rigging, **43**
Overhand throwing technique, 70, **75**
Overhead rescue. *See* Vertical rescue

Paddle hooks, **32, 34**, 94, **96, 115**
Paddles
  proper technique for, 184
  retrieval, 94, **96,** 97
  spare, 18, 49
Paddling, 14–15, 16
Painters
  boat recovery with, 97, **99**
  canoe, 49
  raft recovery with, 54

Patient Assessment System (PAS),
  226–227
Patient care, 176–179
  contact rescue, 177–185
  and evacuation, 185–194
  submerged victims, 181
Pendulum approach rescue, 54, **56,**
  104, 111
Personal safety equipment, 23, **24–35,**
  199
Piggyback ("Pig") rig, 133–134, **135**
Piggyback (two-handed carry), 186,
  189
Pins, 46, 108–109. *See also* Boat pins;
  Pitchpole pin; Vertical pins
Pitchpole pin, **110**
Portaging, **19**
Potholes, 3, **5**, 7, **209**
Potomac River, 1
Preparation, trip, **14–22**, 23
Prijon life jacket, **25**
Prusik, Karl, 214
Prusiks, **24**, 27, **28, 30**, 31–32, 214, **215**
  brake, 130, 132–133
  Telfer lower, 100, **102**
  traveling, 130
  Tyrolean rescue, 147–148
Public-service rescue professionals,
  195–200, 208, 210
  accident prevention, 199
  equipment, 199, 200–204
  jurisdictional conflicts, 197–199
  training and rescue tips, 199–200
Pulley bags, **31**
Pulleys, 31, **34**
  directional, 124, **128, 129, 134, 135**
  simple, 128, **129**
  Telfer lower, 100, 102–106
  traveling, **130–133**
  Z-drag, **128–133**

Radios, 202
Rafts, 41–42, 202, 204
  rescuing swimmers from, **192–194**
  rigging for recovery, 119, 122–**123,**
    125, 134, **136–138**
  self-baling, 42, 119
  self-rescue, **54–56, 62**
  triple-rigged, 42, 43
  use in Telfer lower, 100, 105–106
Ranger crawl, 149, 150
Rappelling, 140–141, **142, 143**

Repair kit, 18
Rescue, overhead or vertical, 139–151, 162
  helicopter, 152–158, 162
Rescue Belt, 94, 95
Rescue craft, 202, 204
Rescue harness, **26, 27, 82,** 114, **116**
  belaying with, 68
Rescue leader, 20, 163, 166, 168–169, 208
Rescue professionals, **195–202,** 208
  equipment, 199, 200–204
  public-service, 195, 200, 210
  steps in river rescue for, 199–200
Rescue ropes, **41**
Rescue teams, 168–170
  base camp, 169, 170
  communication team, 169
  evacuation team, 169
  extrication team, 169
  first aid team, 169
  support team, 169, 170
Rescue 3, 200
Rescue training, 196, 199, 206
  courses, 199, **201**
  "accident scenario," 208, **209**
Rewarming techniques, 182–183
Rigging for pinned boat recovery, 115, 118–135
Righting watercraft, 52–55, 56
River characteristics
  drop and pool, 3, 90
  importance of knowing, 14–16, 196–199
  riverbed make-up, 3
  volume of flow, 3
River classifications, 3, 12–13, 211–212
River evacuation, 186
River hazards, 2, 4–12
  big water, 12, 54
  cold water, 12, 54
  identifying, **196–199**
River professionals, 1, 195, **196,** 208, 210
  management policies, 204–206
  rescue training, 206–208
River signals, **213**
Roll-over lines, 119, 122, **126**
Rolls, Eskimo, **52,** 53
Rope
  ferries, **76–77**
  how to hold, 70, **71**

  rescue by, 64–86, 93–94
  setting rope, **66**–67
  throwing, **66–75**
Rope bags, 202
Rope-coil carry, 186, **191**
Rope-ladder rescue system, 148, 151, **154,** 155
Rope litters, 190, **192**
Rope loops, 81, 82, 100, **132**
Ropes, 23, 38–39, **40–41**
  for bridge lowers, 140
  grab loops, 46, 114, 119
  for haul systems, 38, 124, 130
  kernmantle, 32, 38–39, 41
  Tyrolean rescue, 140, 147
  See also Throw bags
Rope tricks, 115, **116–118,** 122, **123**

Safety, 14–22, 50–51, 139–140, 146, 197, 204
  as factor in rescue system, 167
Safety equipment, 23, **24–35,** 45–49, 199
Saws, 34
Scoop rigs, 202, 205
Scouting, **18–19**
  evacuation route, 190
Sea-anchor haul system, 134, **135,** 202
Self-lowering rescuer system, 149–150, **152**
Self-rescue, **52–63,** 200
Setnika, Tim: *Wilderness Search and Rescue,* 162
Setting rope, **66,** 67
Shock cord, 49
Shore-based lowering system, 151, **153,** 200, 202
Shotover River, 155
Shoulder dislocations, **184–185**
Shoulder straps for carrying litters, 190, **194**
Shuttles, 16
Sidearm throwing technique, 70, 73
Sit harness, 32, 140, **143–145, 149,** 161
Sliding seat lowering system, 149, **151**
Slings, 32
Snag tags, 76, **79–81**
Snubbing system, 124, **127**
Spider boat (cataraft), 42, 100, 204, **207**
Squirt boats, 46
Standing wave, **2**

Steve Thomas rope trick, 122, **123**
Strainers, **2**, 7, **10**
  drill, **14**
  self-rescue, **58, 60**
Strong-swimmer rescues, **81–86**, 111,
  168
Support team, 169, 170
Swamping, 42, 46, 62
  rescue measures for, 46, 62, 97–98
Swiftwater Rescue Belt, **95**
Swimmers, rescuing, **66–71**, 75, **88–94**
Swimming, 53, 54–60, 62–63
  big/cold water, 12
  Capistrano Flip, 55, **56**
  defensive, **57**–60, **63**

Tag-line rescues, 76–81, 168
  floating tag line, **77–79**, 111–112,
    118
  snag tags, 76, **79–81**
  stabilization tag line, 82, **111–112,
    113**
Talus belay, 192, **194**
Telfer lower, 41, 92, **98–106**, 115, 168
  lowering methods, 100–103, **106**
  for patient transport, 186
  rescue, 104–105
  setup, 100, 101
Tension ferry, **85–86**
Tethered boat rescue, 94, **96**
Tethered swimmer rescue, **83**
Thigh braces, 44, 49
Thigh straps, 49, **50**
"Ten Boy Scouts" method haul system,
  126, 127, 128
Thomas (Steve) rope trick, 122, **123**
Throw bags, 23, **24**, 27, **31, 34, 39–40,**
  115
  raft rescues with, 54, **55–56,** 93–94
  throwing techniques, 70, **73, 75**
Throwing rescue, 39, **65–70**, 168
  with belaying techniques, **64**
  for multiple swimmers, 75
  techniques, **66,** 67, **70–75**
Throw ropes, 38–39, **40**
Tow belts, 28–29
Tow system, **24,** 46, **47, 48,** 90, **92**
  boat recovery with, 97–99
  quick-release system, 46, **47, 48, 92**
Traveling pulleys, **130–133**
Trips, river
  choosing paddlers, 16

organization, 16–18
preparation, 14–16, 23
scouting, **18–19**
trip leader, 16, 18, 19, **20–21**
Two-handed carry (piggyback), 186, **189**
Two-man carry, 186, **189**
Tyrolean rescues, 41, 115, 139,
  145–151, 168

UH-1 series helicopter
  landing zone for, 157
Undercut rocks, **2,** 3, 7, **8, 66,** 67
Underhand throwing technique, 70, 73,
  74

Vector pull, 124, **126–128**
Vertical pins, **109–111**
  rescues, 114–115
  rigging for, 115–118
Vertical rescue, 140, 162
  bridge lowers, 115, 139, 140,
    141–145, **159–161**
  helicopters, 152–158, 162
  Tyrolean, **145–151**
V-harness, **101, 103, 104**

Waist belt, 26
Walbridge, Charlie, 22, 53, 57, 155
Watauga River, 108
Water, force of, **214**
Watercraft, 23, 41–49
  See also Boats, decked; Canoes, open;
    Kayaks; Rafts; Rescue craft
Webbing, 32
Wetsuits, **37–38**
"What If" factor, 21–22, 166
Whistles, 34
Whitewater
  hazards, **4–12**
  rating rapids, **12–13,** 21, 211–212
  river characteristics, **2,** 3, 15–16,
    198–199
Wilderness Search and Rescue (Setnicka),
  162
Winches, 126, 146, 202
Wind direction, indicating, 157, **158,**
  221, 222

Z-drag system, 31, 32, **86, 126,
  128–133, 136–137**
  and Tyrolean rescue, 147, **148,**
    149–150, **153**
Zip line rescue, **85–86**

About the AMC

The Appalachian Mountain Club is a nonprofit, volunteer organization committed to conserving natural lands and promoting responsible public use of them. Founded in 1876, it is the oldest conservation and outdoor recreation organization in the country. AMC members were the first to explore and map many areas of the Northeast, and the Club played a vital role in the passage of the Weeks Act, which established the eastern National Forest System.

Activities. Today the AMC conducts an increasingly varied program of outdoor public service. The Club's 35,000 members belong to twelve regional chapters stretching from Maine to Washington, D.C. Each month, chapter volunteers organize and lead hundreds of outdoor trips, workshops, and educational seminars. Club activities include hiking, skiing, climbing, snowshoeing, canoeing, trail building, cycling, and photography. Since 1968, the AMC has offered thousands of inner-city youths the chance to test themselves in the mountains and develop leadership skills through the Youth Opportunities Program. The AMC is also active in environmental research and land-management issues.

Facilities. The Club has built and now maintains many trails, shelters, and camps, a unique system of eight alpine huts in the White Mountains, and the base camp and information center at Pinkham Notch in New Hampshire. Club headquarters in Boston house the nation's largest mountaineering library.

Publications. Beginning in 1907 with the *White Mountain Guide,* the AMC has published authoritative guidebooks and maps to the trails and waterways of the eastern United States. The Club also publishes in the areas of history, ecology, sociology, biography, backcountry management, search-and-rescue, and winter sports, as well as field guides and books for children. *Appalachia,* the nation's oldest mountaineering journal, is published twice a year.

Membership. We invite you to join the AMC. The monthly member's publication, *Appalachia Bulletin,* will keep you informed of Club news, activities, and conservation issues. All members receive discounts on publications and food and lodging in AMC facilities. Membership allows you access to AMC workshops, trips, and other activities, and gives you the satisfaction of supporting the preservation and responsible use of the Northeast's priceless open spaces.

For membership information, call us at (617) 523-0636, or write to:

Appalachian Mountain Club
5 Joy St.
Boston, MA 02108